WHERE THE WEST BEGINS

Essays on Middle Border and Siouxland Writing, in Honor of Herbert Krause

Arthur R. Huseboe and William Geyer
editors

CENTER FOR WESTERN STUDIES PRESS
1978

Cover design by John Carlander, Augustana College
Photograph by William Seward, EROS data Center, Sioux Falls

Library of Congress Catalog Card Number 78-55073
International Standard Book Number 0-931170-02-8.

Printed by Graphic Publishing Co., Inc., Lake Mills, Iowa

CENTER FOR WESTERN STUDIES
AUGUSTANA COLLEGE, SIOUX FALLS, SOUTH DAKOTA 57102

CONTENTS

Herbert Krause 1905-1976

Herbert Krause and the Western Experience

ARTHUR R. HUSEBOE AND WILLIAM GEYER

Herbert Krause would have enjoyed reading through this collection of papers published in his honor. He would not have agreed with the theses in some of them, might have quarreled heartily with a few, and would have grumbled (perhaps) at being included in the company of Archer Gilfillan. But he would have been delighted at rubbing shoulders with his old teacher Ole Rølvaag and with his close friends Manfred and Milton, and he would have been pleased at the idea of a collection of papers that concentrate on the literature of the northern prairies, where his own three novels are set. Above all, Herb Krause would have relished the thought that a chance question of his twenty years ago, uttered out of profound scholarly frustration, should have led by circuitous ways to the publishing of a set of critical essays about the outstanding writers of Siouxland and the Middle Border. "Why can't there be a center," he had asked us in 1958, while doing research on the use of sweet grass in Dakotah religious rites, "where this kind of information can be gotten at easily?"

In the years that followed, the idea of such a research agency ripened in conversations between Krause and his colleagues at Augustana College, and in 1969 the Center for Western Studies was officially organized, with a warmly supportive board of directors and Krause as executive director. From that point on the story of this volume runs quickly to its end. In 1974 the Center published its first book, *Prelude to Glory*, an edition of newspaper accounts of Custer's 1874 expedition to the Black Hills, compiled and introduced by Krause and his colleague Gary Olson. Among the speakers at the testimonial dinner that launched the book that fall was Frederick Manfred, long a supporter of the Center concept, a close friend of Krause, and a near neighbor to the college. Convinced that the Center for Western Studies was now a going concern, Manfred approached the Western Literature Association later that year with the suggestion that the 1977 national convention be held in Sioux Falls, under the sponsorship of the Center and the college. There, Manfred argued, in the heart of Siouxland, was literary wealth aplenty—Rølvaag, Hamlin Garland, Laura

Ingalls Wilder, Krause, John Neihardt, Willa Cather, and others—and the choice of such a locale could give the convention a theme that would stimulate the writing of a great many first-rate papers. The board of directors of the WLA accepted Manfred's recommendation, chose as 1977 president Arthur Huseboe (a member of both the WLA and the Center board), and thus prepared the way for what turned out to be one of the most productive conventions in the Association's twelve-year history.

The essays that came in during 1977 seemed to confirm Manfred's idea that the literature of the northern plains had been steadily growing in interest for a long time and deserved the kind of focus proposed. At the convention that October out of 97 presentations there were no less than 11 on Hamlin Garland (and 6 panelists who discussed his short story "Under the Lion's Paw"), 7 on Rølvaag, 6 on Manfred, 6 on Neihardt, 5 on Cather, and others on middle-border writers like L. Frank Baum, Robert Bly, Gilfillan, Lois Hudson, Krause, Thomas McGrath, Milton, Mari Sandoz, Ruth Suckow, and Wilder. From this wealth came the present collection, winnowed out and bound together by a process that we judge to have been alchemical as well as fortuitous, and justified—in a manner of speaking—as will be shown a little later on.

Krause's peculiar genius qualifies him in at least two other ways as parent of these papers: while as a novelist he captured more brilliantly than any other and in more detail the bittersweet life of the second-generation German immigrant on the northern prairies—thus deserving the attention given him by Steensma and Paulson—as a historian Krause sought always to enlarge the conventional view of the American West beyond its stereotyped or its narrowly national bounds, thus helping to vindicate our inclusion of immigrant sodbusters among the westerners in this collection. It is as novelist, of course, that he is best known. He came suddenly on the scene in 1939 with his first book, *Wind Without Rain*, startling the reviewers and evoking far-flung critical acclaim. For it he won the Friends of American Writers Award and was recommended for the Pulitzer. His second novel, *The Thresher* (1946), required extensive research into steam-powered wheat harvesting in Minnesota and the Dakotas. It was followed by an even more deeply researched novel, *The Oxcart Trail* (1954), set on the St. Paul to Fort Garry overland passage in northwest Minnesota. The next stage in his career—the pursuit of new historical visions of the West—was firmly set.

Very early in his reading, Krause came upon the work of Herbert Bolton, the American historian who more clearly than any predecessor advanced the thesis that United States history can be comprehended only in hemispheric terms. The West, said Bolton, is a region that will be understood only to the degree that we understand the multifarious influences of

Spanish, French, and Anglo-Americans as they interacted over centuries with Native Americans and with one another. The view confirmed what Krause already had come to realize, aware as he was (from his Minnesota vantage point) of the French presence on the plains. The West, Krause now saw, is a vast and rich mosaic of cultural interrelationships that stretch from the mountains of Mexico into the prairies and lakes of Canada over 1500 miles to the northeast. He was led, then, early in his studies, to look deeply into the Spanish and French experiences in western America in search of the sources of early influences which helped in the formation of those social patterns that persist to the present hour.

In an essay that deserves to be more widely known, Krause argues that "such phenomena as the emergence of Chicano self-identity and the eruption at Wounded Knee must have their roots not only in the Anglo-American influenced recent past but in the past of Spanish Oñate and French La Salle, that "if we are to probe the obscurity which surrounds the meaning of the term 'Western' or 'Westerner,' we must be as thoroughly conversant with the western experience from its very beginning as we are with the eastern experience, from Plymouth Rock and Boston to Valley Forge and the westward movement that followed." The gold hunters of the south and the fur traders of the north left centuries of trails for the Americans to follow, but those first Europeans also left behind patterns of reaction between native Americans and white newcomers. "Both Spanish and French yearned for gold," wrote Krause, "remembering Pizzaro and Atahualpa's halls of treasure; gold whether in the earth or on the archtraves of sacred houses. The Spanish found treasure both in the earth and in the templed aisles. Their attitude toward the native generally was one of aloofness, of domination; the Indian was another barrier like earth and stone to block the path to golden fortune. But the French, no less eager for the gold-laid streets beyond the bend in the next stream, found their treasure in a wholly different fashion, running on four feet, as the Indian put it. However, unless the natives, skilled in the craft of trapping, brought the peltries to the French at a central point, the gold still ran on four legs. Thus the French attitude toward the native must have included a reluctant partnership, however temporary, however loosely formed, however expedient." Hence, for Krause, the pattern of human relationships on the plains was that mosaic of culture, formed over centuries, still evident today, and more than ever in need of clearer interpretation.

It is unfortunate that the last research problem to engage his attention was left incomplete, for it would undoubtedly have led Krause to forge still one more link between the French on the northern plains and the Anglo-Americans who succeeded them. Preliminary investigation had encouraged his strong suspicion that the history of the fur trade on the upper Missouri River during the period 1790 to 1840 needs expanding to include a close scrutiny of the activities at the small posts at the headwaters. There it was that much of the significant action took place, according to extant letters and documents in St. Louis, Pierre, and elsewhere. There the policies and practices and even the regulations, purportedly maintained at the larger posts (Fort Tecumseh, Fort Pierre, Fort Union, etc.), were of a different character. There, as Krause wrote, "the action was nakedly uninhibited. Cheating at the headwaters, so to speak, was a microcosm not only of Indian-White relations at the larger posts but also of later agreements and treaties between Indians and white men and formed the genesis and the basis for the troubled amity which exploded in the Little Big Horn and at Wounded Knee and has continued to the present day." Such research, Krause had hoped, would also reveal new aspects of the Anglo-American incursion upon the stage of French and Canadian fur trade activities and the influence of that incursion, commercially and culturally, upon the formation of the growing society on the northern plains.

The geographic focus of Krause's last—and incomplete—historical research was at the western end of the midland expanse that Fred Manfred has christened Siouxland, while Krause's novels are centered in the heart of what Hamlin Garland labeled the Middle Border. Whereas "Siouxland" enjoys the virtue of both breadth and explicitness, being obviously wherever the Sioux lived, Garland's territory is harder to place. Garland answered George Bernard Shaw's question as to what was meant by Middle Border by acknowledging that "in a sense it does not exist and never did. It was but a vaguely defined region even in my boyhood. It was the line drawn by the plow and, broadly speaking, ran parallel to the upper Mississippi when I was a lad. It lay between the land of the hunter and the harvester." What lies between the hunt and harvest of the authors and their scholar-critics in this book is in some ways no more geographically precise. Yet while the title of this collection, *Where the West Begins*, might make our editorial role seem like that of a referee in a boundary dispute, the task has been anything but onerous and frustrating.

For openers we had the enthusiasm, advice, and wisdom of those WLA scholars who met with us at the fall conference and for whom, clearly, the West was not beginning over again, but continuing vigorously—from Siouxland, where we convened, at least as far as the Point Reyes jut into the Pacific. In more than just a manner of speaking, the West for this book began with them. We also had the example of Krause and his insistence that the culture of the Great Plains is and long has been complex and cosmopolitan. And we were convinced that, as there were many romanticisms and numerous versions of the American Dream-Scheme, so there were Wests and beginnings, and that rich pluralism must be a feature of any definition.

The cast of western characters and writers in this little book—a book treating authors of a relatively few plains states—is in fact so diverse in its range as to vindicate Krause's judgment. In one sense, the West of the title is the original Dakota Territory with the lines blurred and amended to bulge no more southerly, easterly, and westerly than what the territorial conscience and imperative of landtakers (even of the literary stripe) would allow. It is Garland's Middle Border, Krause's Pockerbrush, Manfred's Siouxland, the imaginative poetic and political vaulting of Bly and McGrath, the sheep country of Gilfillan, the mythic route crawled and worn by mountain man Hugh Glass and his haunt companyeros, Milton's entry into cycles of continuity within the unconsciousness, Sandoz's Cheyenne country, Rølvaag's and Cather's and Wilder's pioneer land, the long memories and long treks of the Kiowa and the Teton Sioux, and the remembered earth of their historian-poets such as N. Scott Momaday, Black Elk, and Neihardt.

But in the best sense, of course, the western boundaries are inward and the West is a territory of imagination, in a recurring drama of the American character shaped by exigencies of place, then reshaped by subsequent generations who have had to rub strangeness about the past from their eyes to be sure who they were. In that respect the West never recedes but always draws nearer. Consequently, an exactly defined region is less important, we would argue, than the perceptions of the region, than the westering mind itself. This is not to diminish the hold of the writer's environment or the profound wrestle with actuality evoked by the authors represented in this collection. It is rather to give a westerner's notice that truths of the heart are not blazed only along the boundaries of Hawthorne's New England or Faulkner's Mississippi.

The sixteen essays which comprise the remainder of this book provide readers with seasoned and informed guidance to the diverse drama of the region. We are hopeful that the first of them, Robert Steensma's sensitive analysis of Krause's *Wind Without Rain*, may help to reverse his later conclusion that Krause's trio of novels are unlikely to receive much further scholarly attention. For Steensma's introduction to the author, by demonstrating that Krause's unflinching yet poetic vision of rural life on the northern prairies retains vigorous insights, might actually direct and provoke new consideration. Providing additional impetus is Kristoffer Paulson, who, though he finds Krause's second novel, *The Thresher*, too heavy in its foreshadowing, also discovers parallels in theme, structure, and characterization to Ole Rølvaag's *Giants in the Earth*. In its compellingly dark tragedy, the Krause novel like *Giants* achieves for Paulson candid perceptions about power struggles in the West. The affinity of *Giants* to other literature is the subject of Neil T. Eckstein, who examines parallels to the saga tradition in such features as forces of nature endowed in the pioneers' imagination with malevolence and cruelty, the nautical tone of Per Hansa's journey, the brooding fatalism in Beret, and Per's acceptance of fate with honor. This taproot similarity of *Giants* to the saga is one more sign of the complex weave of Rølvaag's art.

If closeness to myth and saga and to vigor and continuity in relation to place characterizes the literature of the northern plains, Christer Mossberg warns that this nearness must be disabused of pastoral idealism, particularly those romantic illusions as to the Edenic circumstances of pioneering. The immigrant diaries, letters, and accounts, which provided writers like Rølvaag with factual bases, dispel such notions. For, as Mossberg clearly shows us, in the complex interpenetration of the two worlds of the immigrant, the plains, which provided room to nourish democratic concepts, allowed just as much space to dilute and diminish the immigrant's old culture, a dilution often played out to the accompaniment of grasshopper plagues and a variety of other hardships. It is interesting, then, that Dolores Rosenblum should discover in her essay on Laura Ingalls Wilder that spatial re-ordering is the chief act of imagination and culture in an immigrant society, thus confirming in the literature what Mossberg found in the diaries and letters. In Wilder's work, the prairie both invites and threatens, the immigrants constantly venture out from and return to the security of little houses, and Wilder's central metaphor for human survival is spatial—filling with human presence the emptiness that threatens to efface humanity. Susan Rosowski finds Willa Cather a denier of romantic definitions and sexist roles for the pioneer woman, arguing that Cather resists prescribing the spatial metaphor to characters merely on the basis of sex, with the pioneer male associated with expansiveness and the female with stability. Instead, Cather's most forceful pioneers, women like Alexandra of *O Pioneers!*, are not bound by traditional stereotypes.

And as to the stern, unromantic realities of life on the plains, we could do no better for an inventory, Austin J. McLean shows, than to turn to the remarkable diary, begun in 1924 by Harding County sheepherder Archer B. Gilfillan. This man of anomalies, who once wrote a scathing review of Krause's *Wind Without Rain*, condemning it for its picture of "stark misery and unrelieved mental anguish," depicts in his own diary an often cheerless encounter with the environment and is mercilessly honest about himself: a Phi Beta Kappa herder of sheep, an incorrigible but inept poker player without equal as an easy mark, a seven-swallow drinker of long habit but less fortitude, a chronic debtor, an inveterate gossiper, a losing battler to starchy obesity, one on whom others practiced lying.

As his most recent novel, *Green Earth* (1977), underscores, Frederick Manfred has helped secure national and international stature for the literature of the northern plains. His accomplishment is measured here in three essays. Peter Oppewall of Calvin College, Manfred's alma mater, treats a period often neglected in analyses of the author, but one influential in his intellectual and emotional development, a biographical chapter in which the biographer's viewpoint and the subject's don't always accord, but in which the tension itself is valuable and instructive. Despite the danger in reading fiction as autobiography, a tracing of the actuality which fed the fiction can, as Oppewall maintains, be crucial to the understanding of an author's developing themes and methods. Anthony Arthur comments that the saga of Hugh Glass, as dramatized in Manfred's *Lord Grizzly*, is as profoundly significant of the American character and experience as *Moby-Dick, Huckleberry Finn,* or *The Great Gatsby*. Epic in that it offers a definition of national character through a protagonist whose adventures exemplify that character, *Lord Grizzly* succeeds by its complete immersion in the speech and the ways of the mountain man, by Hugh's lively sense of social consciousness and by his entering both literally and figuratively into his antagonist. Robert C. Wright likewise shows Manfred's concern for a theme of national significance, one seen as well in writers like Emerson, Whitman, and Faulkner. Manfred points out the paradox that we are separate yet together, isolated but joined, as Wright says, "in transition from the perspective of the individual as isolate to that of the individual as an interlocking member with all living things."

Similarly, William J. Lockwood associates the journeyings in Robert Bly's *Point Reyes Poems* with the middle-border Minnesotan's sense of "the connectedness of things," finding an "unselfconscious sincerity" in the poet's travel to the westernmost edge of the United States. We might add that the self of the seeker, as in Whitman, becomes a representative self in Bly's poems. In one of them, in fact, "November Day at McClure's Beach," analyzed ably by Lockwood, Bly quotes Whitman's *Song of Myself* on animals that do not weep for their sins or lie awake with fitful self-pity. This outward reach of Bly's poetry is paralleled by the political breadth in Thomas McGrath's *Letter to an Imaginary Friend*. Exploring McGrath as communist poet, Frederick C. Stern develops the thesis that "McGrath's politics does for his verse precisely what Eliot's Christianity does for that poet—it provides a framework of conviction and thought and imagery in which he can operate." Paul Pavich reads John R. Milton's recent novel, *Notes to a Bald Buffalo*, as having similar scope, in this case in the exploration of the unconscious. But Milton's is a book which synthesizes through its poetic techniques and paramyth, thus avoiding the view of a fragmented and meaningless world so dominant in contemporary fiction, while binding disparate elements of life with archetypal situations and images.

For those who find little value in Hamlin Garland's fiction after the stark veritism of his middle-border period, Jack L. Davis turns attention to an aspect of Garland frequently missed: his stories between 1895 and 1905 which offer "landmark treatments of the Indians." Rather than retreat romantically, Garland continues his strong social criticism so that, for example, *The Captain of the Gray-Horse Troop* (1902) is an exposure of "cruel, leering racial hate of the border man," which makes the Indian "big game." And if Garland's philosophical military men seem in many ways remote from the actualities of the plains, they are an honest attempt to reconcile the best of two worlds. The tragedy of what cannot be reconciled is the subject of Pam Doher's careful examination of the idioms and figures of Indians in Mari Sandoz's *Cheyenne Autumn*. If the white flood of usurpation made the Cheyenne nation like a crumbling sandbar in the rush of the spring-time Platte, or like one entrapped in a web, we do not wonder that the Cheyenne term for spider, *veho*, was extended to include the white man or that in this autumn of a great people the rich flow of figurative language was to be stemmed. But not entirely stopped. As William Bloodworth shows in the concluding essay, *Black Elk Speaks* and the autobiographical works by N. Scott Momaday are Indian self-expression "practiced with art and eloquence." Neihardt has been both creative and editorial; the book is his, but it is also Black Elk's autobiography, fused with the Sioux visions to become a form of ceremony itself. Momaday in *The Way to Rainy Mountain* gives a personal, poetic articulation of the "remembered earth" of the Kiowa history, tradition, and myth; and even in the more explicitly autobiographical *The Names*, he models his writing after oral stories, with emphasis on "the traditions and people that gave him existence and meaning."

We would be pleased if this book has for you, as it has had for us, just such an emphasis, upon traditions and people that give meaning.

"Our Comings and Goings": Herbert Krause's *Wind Without Rain*

ROBERT C. STEENSMA

Robert C. Steensma, professor of English at the University of Utah, is author of Sir William Temple *(Twayne, 1970).*

The histories of American literature generally ignore the fiction of the North Central plains. Except for brief considerations of, or cursory references to, Ole Rølvaag, Willa Cather, and Hamlin Garland, the novels and short stories about pioneer life in the region have been badly slighted. And in the anthologies of American literature, often produced by the same scholars who write the histories, the same situation prevails, with Cather and Garland the only writers to be represented, and then only with one or two stories each.

Among more recent writers of the area, the case is even worse. Frederick Manfred and Herbert Krause, who have both produced a substantial body of fiction, are never found in the collections. The consequence is that the only northern-plains writer known to a large body of the American public is Laura Ingalls Wilder—and then primarily through a successful television series. This doesn't necessarily detract from the achievement of Mrs. Wilder, but unfortunately the comment of a New York critic, quoted by Willa Cather, still seems to represent the views of many critics and scholars: "I simply don't care a damn what happens in Nebraska, no matter who writes about it."[1]

Cather, Garland, Rølvaag, and Manfred have their champions, of course, but I would like to make a case for Herbert Krause, my teacher and friend, who produced only three novels between 1939 and 1954 while teaching a heavy load of English classes at Augustana and moving on to become a famous regional and national authority in ornithology and western history. The body of his fiction may be small, but his achievement was first-rate as early as his first novel, *Wind Without Rain*, published by Bobbs-Merrill in early 1939, when he was thirty-three. He moved on to write two other novels, each of them distinctive in its own way, in *The Thresher* (1946) and *The Oxcart Trail* (1954).

Before dealing with *Wind Without Rain,* I would like to digress for a moment to outline Herbert Krause's biography as a background for his work. He was born in Fergus Falls, Minnesota (the "Pockerbrush" locale of his first two novels and his book of poetry), on May 25, 1905. He graduated from St. Olaf College in 1933 and then pursued graduate work in English and creative writing at the University of Iowa under Paul Engle and earned his M.A. in 1935. In 1938 he came to Augustana as head of the Department of English and taught courses in Shakespeare, creative writing, American short story and poetry, and literature of the Great Plains. In 1969 he was influential in founding Augustana's Center for Western Studies, of which he became the Director.

In the classroom he was an inspiration to the bright and the seeker, a fearsome mystery to the plodder and the dolt. But more often than not, after an exposure to Professor Krause's humane and concerned wisdom, the dolt became the seeker. I know of a Shakespeare teacher at a western university who, years ago, in Professor Krause's discussion of *Henry IV, Part One*, learned that bluffing an answer to a question on an assigned play as yet unread is not "the better part of valor." In other words, the future academic learned not to play the student Falstaff to Herbert Krause's Prince Hal.

Herbert Krause was not only an outstanding teacher, but also the true scholar in the best sense of the phrase. In addition to his fiction-writing, he was an expert and inveterate birdwatcher whose articles found print in important ornithological journals and in O. S. Pettingill's book, *Birdwatcher's America.* And he moved just as comfortably in western American history, writing the Minnesota centennial poem, "Giant in the Wooded North," and, with Gary Olson, the highly regarded historical book, *Prelude to Glory.* Again, like the true scholar, he was not content to share his knowledge with a small audience; he was a Fulbright lecturer at the universities of Witwatersrand and Natal in South Africa and a Rockefeller Foundation visiting professor at the University of the Philippines. He moved easily as a friend to a number of important American writers, among them Robert Frost, Stephen Vincent Benet, Paul Engle, Frederick Manfred, and Wallace Stegner. But despite his conversance with the great world beyond the prairies and the campus, he was always the friend of both student and colleague. By the time of his death on September 22, 1976, he had become in the minds of several Augustana generations the embodiment of the renaissance man.

Thus the man—and now to his first novel, which, to my mind, is the best of the three he published. *Wind Without Rain*, which runs to 364 pages, is set in the so-called "Pockerbrush" country (a name, so far as I know, invented by Krause) of west-central Minnesota, about 150 miles northwest of Minneapolis-St. Paul and about 50 miles east of the Dakota line, in the early years of this century. The story is told by Jepthah Vildvogel, an invalid who looks back upon his childhood and youth on the family farm near Fergus Falls and the fictional Mary's Hill with bitter and puzzling memories of the events surrounding the five other members of his family: Johann the father, Minna the mother, and three brothers—Walter and Fritzie (older) and Franz (younger). They live upon an eighty-acre tract, from which they wring a penurious and bitter living.

The father is harsh in manner and sour in temperament, his marriage marred by suspicions of his wife's fidelity and Franz's paternity. The mother is fearful and shrinking, clinging to her sons, her religious beliefs, and those few moments of peace when her husband is away from home. Walter, the eldest son, has begun to take on the ways of his father. Fritzie, the second-born, fights against the dreariness and disappointments of the farm with pranks and humor. The third son, Jepthah (often called Jeppie), is the perceptive one, and the youngest, Franz, is drawn to beauty in all its forms, whether in flowers, in music or a golden braid of hair.

Franz, growing up through a traumatic adolescence, is attracted to two girls, Tinkla Bauer and Liliem Schoen, who are as opposite as two young women can be. Tinkla is robust physically and spiritually, embodying all that is necessary to a hard-working farm wife, while Liliem (whose name and actions suggest the Talmudic Lilith, who was Adam's wife before he married Eve and who became the mother of demons) is fickle, carefree, and exotically beautiful with her golden hair. Franz is forced to marry the pregnant Tinkla while he is still in love with Liliem, and his continuing love for her brings about the catastrophe of the novel. He accidentally runs over and kills his young daughter, Theodora, while he is trying to escape what he thinks is an arresting sheriff, a mistake created in part by his agony at finding Liliem in bed with Jonas Bluber in a sleazy resort cabin. Another catastrophe is the accidental crippling of Jepthah at a sledding party, for which Franz holds himself guilty.

By the end of the story, the father and mother are both dead, never really reconciled to each other and never free from debt; Walter, snared in a shotgun marriage, has moved away; Jepthah is crippled in both body and spirit; and Fritzie has followed the agricultural frontier into the Dakotas. All have been defeated by the cruel life of the farm, by the inexplicable and whimsical forces of Nature and life, and by their own hungers and needs. All have come to feel with Jepthah that life is too often "Black frost in summertime and the crop dead on the stalk,"[2] a predicament in which men and women asked "for song and received only sorrow" (p. 14), in which they might as "well cry out against the grave, twisting the heart's agony over the clods," a painful dilemma in which life, like the Vildvogel father, commands "our yeas and nays, even to our comings and goings" (p. 70).

Although the narrator is the now older, crippled, and embittered Jepthah, who looks "back now, quietly from this white interlude of peace" (p. 11), the central character is Franz, who at the beginning of the novel is seven years old and at the end somewhere in his twenties, his life ruined and his spirit deadened by the memories of his cruel father, the crippling of Jepthah, his forced marriage to the stolid Tinkla, the death of the beloved daughter, and ugly smashing of his image of Liliem. The music of his soul, poured out by his fiddle in the lilting *Barcarolle* and the bitter-sweet *Liebeslied* on many occasions, has died. He fulfills the almost prophetic remark made by Jepthah very early in the book: "always after this night Franz would remember beauty and pain as two that go together, balancing on the pivot of experience, like two buckets, pulling at the ends of the wooden yoke Mother put on her shoulders when she carried water from the pasture spring" (p. 40).

The theme of *Wind Without Rain* is the struggle and defeat of a proud and sensitive young man at the hands of circumstance and his youthful hunger for love and beauty. Franz is a boy unsuited for the unremitting toil of the farm. Unlike his father and his three brothers, he finds no meaning in the dirty rigors of barn and field. Instead he finds his fulfillment in the old fiddle inherited from Old Lindergaard and in the yellow hair of Liliem Schoen.

Certainly *Wind Without Rain* might be read from other perspectives. The social historian of the farming frontier would find a treasure-trove of customs and manners, the folklorist a wide variety of games, square-dance songs, and folk beliefs. The book weaves together many rich strands into an evocative statement about farm life which frequently recalls the best of Rølvaag, Cather, and Garland, three novelists who probably played an important role in the development of Herbert Krause's art and his vision of life.

In unfolding the tragedy of Franz Vildvogel, the author employs three symbols which recur again and again to represent the forces pulling at the heart of the young boy: music (as in the flute, the fiddle, the player-organ, and the two songs, *Barcarolle* and *Liebeslied*), the dances and parties at which the farmers gather on important occasions, and Mason's Resort (and in juxtaposition to it, the church). Each is important to spiritual destruction of Franz, and each serves as a focus for the action of the story.

From the very beginning of the novel Franz is depressed by the conditions on the farm, a view shared by Jepthah:

> Change crept like a beggar over our farm, slowly and with no more hurry than rust. . . . The house wanted paper, and the barn glass instead of rags for windows, but there never seemed money for nails or putty to stop a crack ("Use clay," ordered Father), and the fences got

> down and lost in the burning bushes. We learned to expect corn meal and potatoes twice a day and rye brew when the coffee failed. We took it, though, as we took measles or the heifer's dropping a dead calf—something that couldn't be shouldered aside any more than the hog-back knolls or a thunderbolt. . . . I remember the tiredness of Mother's eyes, the violet-blue in them fading to no color at all (pp. 18-19).

Franz tries to escape from this grim reality in the pleasures of the senses. He is the only brother who appreciates any kind of beauty. Struck by the loveliness of Liliem when she first visits the Vildvogel farm as a child, "Franz stared and stared at her with a puzzled wonder, as though she weren't real." A few moments later he gently pulls off her cap, fascinated by her golden curls, and "put a finger on them as if they were hummingbirds and no more tangible to nerve-ends than the pale ghost candles in the marsh. Softly, with tenderness" (p. 28). Later, when they fall in love as teenagers, she gives him a braid of her hair as a memento of their love.

But it is music, both in the forms of song and instrument, which fascinates him and gives meaning to his life. Very early in his childhood he whirls ecstatically to Jaahcobs' accordion (p. 24), and a short while later he is so enchanted by Mr. Grieber's rendition of "Ich weiss nicht was soll es bedeuten" on the flute that he innocently tries to steal the instrument for his own pleasure, a deed for which his father strikes him brutally (pp. 39-40). And he takes endless delight in the player-organ brought home by his father, endlessly cranking the machine to play *Barcarolle* and other waltzes (pp. 59-60).

Later he inherits the fiddle from Old Lindergaard and teaches himself to play it, in the process becoming a popular guest at the barn dances at neighboring farms, although he puts it aside when he judges himself guilty for the crippling of Jepthah in the sledding accident: "The fiddle strings cracked themselves loose on the bridge, untouched now, though more than once Franz made as if to put resin on the bow, but let the cover down slowly and headed for the door" (p. 121). But, to ease his self-imposed guilt and his love dilemma over Tinkla and Liliem, he begins playing again, almost always the sad strains of *Liebeslied*: "Then the fiddle joined the robin, softly and yet with a cry in the strings, carrying melody into the room—and beyond—beyond the rooftops to the sky. Wood-smell and the lullaby of *Liebeslied*, Franz letting his fingers say aloud what was too deep to be caught and held to view by a mere net of words" (pp. 162-163). But always the effect of his playing is magical for the country folk:

> But no one missed a sound—the sad, heartbroken cry of *Liebeslied* wailing between them, joining them. He played, a sadness deep and lonely as desert places quavering in the strings; something inside him

> going to pieces; an inner grief plowed and harrowed with the implements of fear, and wild surgings tearing in him like untamed colts, bridle-free and stranger to a furrow; eyes blinkered with shadow and his hair more unkempt with every leap of the bow.
>
> The shouting among the dancers died; quiet grins changed to the ghosts of smiles. . . . Men pressed closer to their partners, and arms that had been slack grew tight with yearning, with a kind of fear of losing what they held. . . . The musky pungence of hay and wild rose gave off fragrance and dew, drifting in to become part of the melody—hay that tomorrow or next week would pile high where now the dancers listened, forgetful of calluses and the hard mornings and afternoons waiting for them; consciously only of softness in their arms and the wild honey of madness leaping under the skin (p. 263).

Franz's impassioned music here is the consequence of hearing a few moments before that Liliem is engaged to Jonas.

But by the end of the story, after he had lost Liliem to sexual license and his daughter to his own panic, the fiddle sings a coda of anguish, catharsis, and dim hope: "The fiddle sang with a loneliness even beyond tears. But under the grief, like crumbly ledge-rock under hills, lay strength, I thought; crumbly but holding together. And hope, however moldy and moth-eaten. Or so it seemed. . . . The fiddle was still now, still as the early night, the day a closed chapter, and the heart too tired to wonder about tomorrow" (p. 364).

Music thus serves Franz as escape, as expression of joy and sorrow, as sustenance to his soul, and as expiation for sins, both real and imagined. But he is always aware that his secular music is considered frivolous in the eyes of his father and profane in those of the Lutheran pastor, that *éminence grise* who refuses to permit the burial of Old Lindergaard the fiddler in hallowed ground. It is also the pastor who, while visiting the Vildvogel home for Sunday dinner, throws the *Barcarolle* roller into the fire: "Bruder Vildvogel—in this place—Devil's tunes—and you fresh from the house of God. . . . Burn it; burn the wood of the Devil" (p. 63).

Franz is haunted by Grandma Katzenhoff's folktale of the great lord, the demonic fiddler in the red cloak, and the murder of the lord as the satanic figure gloats, "The E-string—it got him—the E-string" (p. 73). A few moments after the old lady's story, Franz's own E-string breaks: "Franz watched the broken string-end dangling, jerking in the air, and looked as if a ghost had put a cold hand on his shoulder" (p. 75). Some years later, after learning of Liliem's engagement to Jonas, he first tauntingly plays *The Girl I Left Behind Me*, then *Liebeslied*—and then the E-string breaks again, a foreshadowing of the tragedy which ends the book (p. 263).

Related to the symbols of music are those of the dances and parties at which the hardworking farmers gather to escape the rigors and disappointments of their occupation and to celebrate important community events such as marriage and confirmation. At these dances, under the influence of the music, the drink, and his own hot blood, Franz courts both Liliem and Tinkla (his preference clearly for Liliem) and suffers the agonies of first love and love lost. It is at the Prinzings' barn-dance that he earns his first money—a dollar—as a musician, though a heavy rain keeps the crowd small and though he must turn the money over to his bank-haunted father (pp. 82-83).

When Fritzie is confirmed in the Lutheran Church, a confirmation party is held at the Prinzings', and Franz is invited to participate in a fiddling contest with the much older and more experienced Arne Flederman and Heinrich Muehlbank (though the former does not show up). The two men go at it, but the older is no match for the younger; he puts away his instrument and admits, "No use of me making a fool of myself. The beer is yours, Franz" (p. 185). And it is after the contest, in a game of Post Office, that we see the anguished love of Franz for both women; he kisses Tinkla boisterously on the lips and Liliem chivalrously on the hand (p. 187).

And, sometime later, Franz is expecting to take Liliem to yet another dance, but she breaks the date and angrily demands that he return the braid of hair she had previously given him. Heartbroken, he takes Tinkla instead, but almost ignores her as he fiddles madly and desperately watches the door, hoping for the appearance of Liliem. On the way home, however, he snuggles close to Tinkla, "half-forgetting Liliem in the nearness of Tinkla" (p. 205).

At the next dance—at the Mortons'—it becomes clear that Liliem is in his blood more than ever. They taunt each other through Tinkla, but he takes Tinkla home while Jepthah rides in the back seat. Jepthah senses, as does Tinkla, that Franz's heart belongs to Liliem, and he recalls with a sickness of heart what he overheard earlier in the evening—Liliem making love to Jonas in a wagon parked in a remote part of the yard. Jepthah also senses that Liliem can only destroy Franz, and he ponders the meaning of it all: "I wondered if there were surety in heaven or earth for hope. This blind staggering for all of us. . . . But in that homeward ride, I dreaded tomorrow and the day after, with the blind dread of an animal" (p. 242).

At still another dance at the Prinzings', Franz is again first fiddler, but it is at this dance that he learns of Liliem's engagement. In his frenzied playing the E-string breaks, signifying the death of Liliem's love for him and the approaching tragedy. As the dance ends, the spiritual darkness deepens as Diah Kloster murders Minica Morton as the result of a love-rivalry (pp. 255-264, passim).

The dances are the emotional crests of Franz's life. To each of them he goes for music and dance, for laughter, and for the company of a girl. At each of them he experiences both ecstasy and anguish—but never boredom. The music, the laughter, the warm flesh—all help him escape the tyranny of the farm, his father, the pastor, and the bad memories.

The third symbol in the book, though not as pervasive as music or the dance, is Mason's Resort, at which only one major scene takes place, that of Franz's shattering disillusionment with Liliem. Even though the resort is not mentioned until almost midway through the book, it becomes a magnet to the wild young people, "another Sodom and Gomorrah" to the pastor, and a symbol of debauchery contrasted to the rather simple pleasures of the barn-dances. Only Jonas the playboy, Liliem the coquette, and Leff Sperry the bootlegger are drawn to the place. Franz will have nothing to do with it, but when he finally goes there unwillingly in the company of Leff, his world, as he idealizes it in Liliem, is destroyed.

Mason's Resort, then, symbolizes the degenerative influence that destroys the homely virtues found in the Pockerbrush farmers. They are generally honest, just, hardworking, persevering, each in his or her own way, though not without occasional and substantial failings. Their Lutheran Christianity, as represented in the pastor and his sermons, tends to be harsh and rigid, opposed to art and the lighter aspects of life, as Franz comes to realize, "that laughter and fiddle music stayed outside when the church door banged" (p. 191). The pastor, calling upon the family after Jepthah's accident, provides no comfort; he simply says, "Evil, that's what at the root of sickness and accidents and the frailties of the flesh. Sin and the Devil, carrying you off to the torture chambers of Hell. Think about it. . . . You have time, lying there. Blessed hours of Grace. A gift of God. Good day" (p. 142). But the theological and personal austerity of the pastor is contrasted sharply with the simple and loving piety of Franz's mother, who finds comfort in her Bible, her book of Biblical stories, and her strong faith.

Thus the people of *Wind Without Rain* are caught between the worlds of the flesh and the spirit. Some, like Jonas, Liliem, and Leff, lose their souls in pursuit of pleasure. Others—most, in fact—move through their rounds of almost endless work, struggles with crops and weather and the ever-threatening bank, and whatever pleasures they can snatch at the parties and dances. And some—like Pete Prinzing, castrated by the Schaaf family to avenge the sexual wrong to their daughter, and Diah Kloster, who murders a love-rival (Minica Morton) in a moment of drunken passion—are destroyed. Of this latter group are also Franz, tragically flawed by his illicit longing for Liliem, and the crippled Jepthah, who bitterly observes at one point,

> I wondered sometimes; about the farm enclosing us like a pen in which to run our scraggly lives; and was plagued in dubious moments with a great Why—the why of fiddle tunes and laughter, and the grimness Father alone understood, looking at Franz; the patience of Mother's hands; the crutches, no flesh and bone, but walking as legs. . . . Why? Why? Wondering how it would end and suspecting it never would; unless there is finality with sight and sound stopped up with death (p. 206).

And years later, looking back on it all, as he begins telling the story, he understands only a little more: "I can look back now, from this white interlude of peace, and see as one from a far hill how all our days were spent. Wasted in a sort of hen-fight to snatch from life a moldy rind of happiness, avoiding when we could the nettle-patches of hurt" (p. 11).

Thus Herbert Krause presents a grim and realistic picture, a deeply moving one, of farm life on the North Central plains. *Wind Without Rain* is a vision of existence in which the people, all of them first- or second-generation immigrants, battle against the elements and themselves to establish themselves in a new land. Like Rølvaag, Cather, and Garland, he does so without resorting to the melodramatic claptrap which has cluttered so much of the fiction about midwestern farm life. As in Rølvaag's best work there is the sensuous appreciation of Nature, a rhythmic and poetic style, and an awareness of the tragedy that life sometimes brings to those who test their strength against it. Like Willa Cather, Herbert Krause shows a deep admiration for the human capacity for suffering and its fight for survival. And, as in the early work of Garland, there is the permeating and stifling sense of the casualties inflicted upon the minds, bodies, and spirits of the pioneers.

Herbert Krause is perhaps closest to Rølvaag (whom he knew at St. Olaf before Rølvaag's death in 1931), for much of what occurs in *Wind Without Rain* is internalized, much of the power deriving from the psychological reactions of the characters, particularly Franz and Jepthah, rather than the episodes themselves. Much of the tension in the Vildvogel household, for example, is the consequence of the father's nagging suspicions of his wife's relationship with a hired man (and the possible bastardy of Franz) and his own memories of his jail term many years before. This is the kind of thing that Rølvaag does so well in making credible the forces working on Beret (particularly in *Giants in the Earth*) and Peder Victorious (in *Peder Victorious* and *Their Fathers' God*). In both Rølvaag and Krause we sense, as we do in Cather but rarely in Garland, a powerful thrust of life, something that Virginia Woolf heard in Turgenev: "the hum of life in the fields; a horse champs his bit; a butterfly circles and wheels."[3]

As I suggested at the beginning of this paper, *Wind Without Rain* has been ignored by the critics except during the first few months after its publication, when it was reviewed in *The Saturday Review of Literature* (February 11, 1939), *The New York Times* (February 12), *The Nation* (February 18), *The New Republic* (March 8), and the *Times Literary Supplement* (July 15). One review was strongly and archly negative; another was enthusiastically positive; the others were cautious and mixed in their reactions.

In the interest of time I will quote from only two—the strongly unfavorable and the very positive. Writing in *The New Republic*, Miriam Borgenicht speaks of *Wind Without Rain* as "364 pages of sustained grimness" in which if "anyone smiles here, you can be sure that tomorrow some poor fellow will suffer for it." She goes on to fault the novelist for achieving his effect "by piling image on image and word on word. Mr. Krause puts as much into the monotony of an evening at home as into a violent accident."[4]

On the other hand, Wallace Stegner, who had won a prize for his own first novel (*Remembering Laughter*) several years before, was much more sympathetic in *The Saturday Review of Literature*. Stegner calls it "one of the best first novels in a good many years," though the story "will not please those who inhale literature as hasheesh, nor those who read to have their comfortable superstitions ratified." Admitting that it "is not a comforting book," he says that is it nevertheless "a very beautiful novel . . . beautiful in the *how* of its writing. Herbert Krause was poet before he turned novelist. He is still a poet here, clairvoyantly sensitive to the evocative power of language." And Stegner concludes that Krause can, "without compromising in the least the integrity of his observation, or softening his picture of the world, still transmute that real world into beauty."[5] The editors must have agreed with Stegner's assessment, for Herbert Krause's picture was featured on the cover of the magazine.

I must admit that there is little likelihood that Herbert Krause's fiction will receive much further attention from critics and scholars. And yet in his book of poems and in his three novels, I believe that his achievement was great and that his work proves the truth of what Willa Cather once said: "A man must live and know and labor and endure before he can write a book that purports to tell of life."[6]

The great world may know little of Herbert Krause's fiction, but to those of use who were his students and colleagues and whose own ancestry is rooted in the northern European immigration to the North Central plains in the latter half of the nineteenth century, his work reminds us of where we came from. As Herbert Krause sums it up in one of his own poems,

So much
Forgotten comes back, so little back to keep,
Waking, perhaps, or clouding in sleep.[7]

Truly, *Wind Without Rain* is a significant and evocative novel in the literature of the American West, for it is a graphic reminder of our human comedy, "our comings and goings," in which, all too often, "beauty and pain go together."

Notes

1. Willa Cather, *On Writing* (New York: Knopf, 1949), p. 31.
2. Herbert Krause, *Wind Without Rain* (Indianapolis: Bobbs-Merrill, 1939; Sioux Falls, South Dakota: Brevet Press, 1976), p. 35.
3. Virginia Woolf, "The Novels of Turgenev," *The Captain's Death Bed and Other Essays* (New York: Harcourt, 1950), p. 59.
4. Miriam Borgenicht, *The New Republic*, March 8, 1939, p. 144.
5. Wallace Stegner, "A Strong Novel of the Minnesota Land," *Saturday Review of Literature*, February 11, 1939, p. 5.
6. Willa Cather, at age twenty, as quoted in E. K. Brown, *Willa Cather: A Critical Biography* (New York: Knopf, 1970), p. 67.
7. Herbert Krause, "By April Waters Years Away," *Neighbor Boy* (Iowa City: Midland House, 1939), p. 43.

Ole Rølvaag, Herbert Krause, and the Frontier Thesis of Frederick Jackson Turner

KRISTOFFER F. PAULSON

Kristoffer F. Paulson, associate professor of English at Simon Fraser University, British Columbia, has written on Rølvaag for Norwegian-American Studies *and for* Ole Rølvaag: Artist and Cultural Leader *(1975).*

Frederick Jackson Turner constantly emphasizes the optimism of the frontier-formed character; America is another name for opportunity. Doing, taking, moving, conquering and growing are the foundation stones and the joys of the American dream. But invariably Turner's list of optimistic actions contains the warning of the dangers in "pressing individual liberty beyond its proper bounds. . . ."[1]

Per Hansa in Ole Rølvaag's *Giants in the Earth* and Johnny Black in Herbert Krause's *The Thresher* reflect the Turner thesis that the frontier formed a distinct American character, but both novelists emphasize the darker elements of the thesis and its muted warnings. Krause's view of the formulative force of the frontier appears much darker than Rølvaag's, but the difference is more stylistic than thematic or structural. Rølvaag uses a combination of romance and realism, playing one off against the other to develop and elevate the paradoxical nature of Per Hansa and to increase the dramatic intensity of the novel. Krause uses straight realism covered by a heavy gloom of fully foreshadowed and then fully realized catastrophe that is frequently too pat and sometimes sentimentally overplayed.[2] Thematically, frontier opportunity becomes the game of power for both Per Hansa and Johnny Black; structurally, the novels are the same: initial struggle, subsequent conquest but at tremendous psychological and spiritual cost, and final tragedy. The novels share a tragic vision of America.

Turner submerges the potential dangers of the American character formed by the frontier in a well of buoyant exuberance and definite admiration for rugged American individualism, but just as certainly he recognizes it as a potential force for evil as well as for good:

That coarseness and strength combined with acuteness and inquisitiveness; that practical, inventive turn of mind, quick to find expedients; that masterful grasp of material things, lacking in the artistic but powerful to effect great ends; that restless, nervous energy; that dominant individualism, working for good and evil, and withal that buoyance and exuberance which comes with freedom (p. 37).

All of these dominant American frontier traits, the exuberance, the inventive practicality, the restlessness, and the nervous energy are abundantly evident in the actions of both Per Hansa and Johnny Black. Per Hansa conceives of his quarter section of Dakota prairie as a kingdom straight from "a wondrous fairy tale—a romance in which he was both prince and king. . . . These days he was never at rest . . . nothing tired him out here."[3] Johnny Black's will to work and his restless energy are obvious and constant: "Johnny rushed from engine to separator, from Snoose and the tank wagon to Alb and the grain spout, as though he were a dozen people."[4]

Energy, restlessness, work. Turner lays his finger carefully on these traits of American character. The man on the frontier "turned his attention to the great task of subduing [the frontier] to the purpose of civilization, and to the task of advancing his economic and social status in the new democracy. Art, literature, refinement, scientific administration, all had to give way to this titanic labor. Energy, incessant activity, became the lot of the new American" (p. 211). The actions of Per Hansa and Johnny Black appear as individual dramatizations of Turner's general observations. Per Hansa "could not be still for a moment": "a divine restlessness ran in his blood; he strode forward with outstretched arms toward the wonders of the future. . . . " (p. 109, my ellipsis). As hard as Johnny Black drives his men on the threshing crew, they cannot "help viewing him with a grouchy sort of admiration": "night after night they'd be snoring before he blew the lantern . . . . he was the first to strike a match and shake the fireman into wakefulness" (p. 275).

Per Hansa has a very "practical, inventive turn of mind" (Turner, p. 37). He breaks more prairie than his neighbors, trades with the Indians, and grows rich as he provides for his family and the community through hard work and practical ingenuity. He builds his house and barn together, giving him winter-warmth and a head start over his neighbors in getting a crop planted the first season. In secret he weaves a Lofoten fish net that catches pickerel in the Sioux River and ducks in the swamps west of his homestead. With calculated modesty he presents some of his catch to his neighbors much as a king sends around presents to his less fortunate peers. When the neighbors arrive to ask him how he secured the ducks, Per Hansa sits "enjoying his little triumph" at their "amazement" with the white-washed walls inside his sod house. Hans Olsa recognizes that Per Hansa is changing on the frontier. Hans Olsa gazes at Per Hansa a long time to see if this is really the same man that he knew in Norway and then says quietly, but with deliberation: "You have made it pretty fine inside, Per Hansa; but. . . . You shouldn't be vain in your own strength, you know" (pp. 196-97, my ellipsis).

Beret, too, recognizes and fears the exuberant optimism, churned by a will that refuses to be thwarted at the core of Per Hansa's character: "Now it had taken possession of him again—that indomitable, conquering mood which seemed to give him the right of way wherever he went, whatever he did. Outwardly at such times, he showed only a buoyant recklessness . . . . but down beneath all this lay a stern determination of purpose, a driving force, so strong that she [Beret] shrank from the least contact with it" (p. 41, my ellipsis).

To depict the rise of Per Hansa to the position of leader and king within the community, Rølvaag weaves the characteristics of the Askelad, hero of the Norwegian folk-tale, into the characterization of Per Hansa. In the folk-tales the Askelad finds the path to the fairy castle, kills the trolls, saves the princess, and inherits the kingdom. Per Hansa does find the path to the Dakota kingdom, and later he does find the lost cattle, and he does drive off the Irish trolls. The reader is swept up in the romance of the folk-myth and accepts Per Hansa's realistic success as tangible proof of the dream of American opportunity. Rølvaag incorporates his knowledge of the Viking sagas and the works of Norwegian authors during Norway's nineteenth-century romantic movement into his creation of Per Hansa's realistic actions, giving them a quality and stature that are epic—or tragic. Rølvaag's pessimism and tragic vision are muted, particularly in the first book of *Giants*, "The Landtaking," because he blends the very realistic actions of Per Hansa and the myths of the Norwegian folk-tale with the optimism, energy, ambition and recklessness one associates with the American character formed by the frontier.

Johnny Black is Turner's frontier thesis in spades: the ambition, the strength, the energy, the recklessness, and the defiance of all restraints are the essentials of his character. The exuberance and the buoyance are many times apparent, but almost invariably qualified with a defensive shield of defiance that colors the tone of the actions to one of dark, depressing, and dangerous black. The drive for power, so frequently romanticized and therefore overlooked in Rølvaag's *Giants*, is specific, open, and raw in Krause's *The Thresher*. The most revealing example is the first time Johnny Schwartz drives the horse power of Uncle Herm's threshing rig, the climactic action that concludes Johnny's adolescence:

> Suddenly Johnny laughed. . . . He stood, free and easy beside the whip. Even then, this first time his legs spread commandingly over the wheeling iron, he was blindly aware of something in his hands

> (not tangible as leather is or fork handle oak), something that was more potent than whip or club or bulging shoulders.
> . . . . Power—power which spun iron and lifted shakers, which ripped the coffined life of the wheat from the husk and poured grain from the spout into the buckets in the tally box. Power which was deaf to any thought. . . . "I'm the boss," he exulted. . . . They're going to come crawlin' to me." . . . . Power—and it lay under his hand, at the touch of a whip, in a bark from his throat (pp. 167-68).

Powerful and even terrifying the passage captures almost perfectly the essential character of Johnny Black: the ambition and the energy, the confidence and the ability, the defiance and the ruthlessness: "They're going to come crawlin' to me." Pride he has had from the very beginning and he becomes ever more pride-filled. His frequently sensitive thoughts do not soften his naked drive for power and his desire to succeed, to crush, to conquer and subdue.

Having digested this passage on power the reader can believe any of Johnny's later actions. He pulls his threshing rig out of Amos Timmerman's field over a price dispute with ruthless calculation, leaving the stacks to rot, refusing to reconsider his action when Timmerman capitulates: " 'That'll show 'em,' he exulted" (p. 425). He changes his name from the German "Schwartz" to American "Black" in the face of the German-American community's sneers and even Uncle Herm's bitterness: "Schwartz was my friend. . . . Go ahead, spit in your own well, if you think the water will be any fresher" (p. 256). The reader can even believe the absolute insensitivity and frenetic perversity of Johnny Black's refusal to allow his faster team of "matched blacks" to be unhitched from the tank wagon to carry the dying Snoose, Johnny's only real friend, to the doctor (pp. 324-25). Lilice's entreaties to give up threshing fall on deaf ears, and her increasing insanity may devastate his thoughts, but won't change his actions. Johnny Black is not insensitive to other people's natures or actions; he is extremely sensitive, but his sensitivity is rarely transformed into the concerned act. He can regret an action, as he does frequently, but he cannot change. He suppresses his thought and emotions in work and action: "Work, that's what you needed when thinking pressed too hard on you" (p. 110).

Johnny Black conquers. He works for Bory Tetzell and learns all there is to know about threshing, and develops a lifetime hatred for Tetzell, his rival. Johnny becomes Uncle Herm's fireman and takes over the steam rig before he is twenty. From then on he rises steadily in power and influence as he acquires first the "Red Star," then the "Buffalo Head," and finally the "Golden Bird" with driver wheels "higher than most men were tall, as wide as a young man's chest" (p. 401). All three of these steam threshing rigs toot defiance to the world and to Bory Tetzell during the threshing runs of the good years. Johnny Black's ambition, will, and pride know no bounds; he reaches his pinnacle of power and position; he crushes all opposition, rival threshers and farmers alike. He has three huge threshing rigs, the prized Norton contract, and he holds the mortgage on Bory Tetzell's one threshing rig: "Triumphant, Johnny grinned over the steering wheel. . . . No use in denying it, he had his world by the tail and was swinging it. . . . The farmers were not far from their knees to get his outfits to thresh in their yards. . . . And Bory Tetzell had had a taste of his knuckles." The truism that "economic power secures political power" (Turner, p. 32) holds true on whatever level of economic power one describes. And power, of course, corrupts; given Johnny Black's pride, exultation, and triumph, the reversal, the fall, and the catastrophe are inevitable.

Per Hansa's desire for power is not nearly so blatant, but make no mistake, his craving is just as stong, willful, and successful as Johnny Black's and finally, just as destructive. Several incidents in *Giants* reveal Per Hansa's "indomitable, conquering mood which seemed to give him the right of way, wherever he went, whatever he did" (p. 41). In the midst of his reverie of the fairy tale kingdom he is building on the Dakota prairie, he stumbles across the landmarks put down by the Irish settlers the previous fall, stakes with strange, outlandish names he'd never seen. The Irish, the reader finds out later, have no legal claim to the land because they have not filed on their claims. Per Hansa has no certain knowledge of this fact, but he realizes that the Irish have obviously been there prior to the Norwegians' arrival that spring. And he knows the Irish will return to claim the land.

Per Hansa romanticizes his actions; the Irish become the trolls of the Norwegian folk-myth and he the Askelad with the magic sword: "Before his thoughts stood ever the same problem: How would it be when the trolls came? [. . .] all his strength would be needed to wield the enchanted sword. . . . For these would be archtrolls, no less" (p. 121, my ellipsis in brackets). But there is nothing romantic about his actions. Revealing his discovery to no one, he removes and burns the landmarks, filling the stake holes with growing sod plugs: "it was going to be hard to see that *here* a stake had ever been standing!" (p. 118).

Per Hansa's secret, swift and practical solution is perfectly in keeping with frontier character, "quick to find expedients" (Turner, p. 37). And Per Hansa's later action, confronting the Irish settlers face to face, parallels exactly what Turner says about typical American frontier law:

> The frontiersman was impatient of restraints. He knew how to preserve order, even in the absence of legal authority. If there were cattle thieves, lynch law was sudden and effective. . . . Substantial justice, secured in the most direct way was the ideal of the backwoodsman.

. . . He had little patience with the finely drawn distinctions or scruples of method. If the thing was proper to be done, then the most immediate, rough and ready, effective way was the best way (p. 212).

The Irish settlers do return to claim the land, and substantial and immedicate "justice" is what Per Hansa metes out to the Irish homesteaders and what he demands from his Norwegian friends. Hans Olsa, slow to comprehend the real threat to his land, pauses to ponder the problem and says that the government should clear up the rival claims. Per Hansa, impatient to get things settled, demonstrates by his answer that the frontier is already changing his old country attitudes: " 'Why certainly,' said Per Hansa, with shrewd common sense. . . . 'The government is all right in its place—no one questions that! But out here this morning, the government is a little too far away . . . that's where the trouble comes in' " (p. 137, Rølvaag's ellipsis).[5] And so the confrontation between the Norwegians and the Irish takes place. The fight is nasty, brutish, and short: or, epic, exhilarating, patriotic, righteous, and short, depending on your realistic or romantic point-of-view or on your religious and nationalistic predilections. The Irish relinquish their claims to the Norwegian land and move a couple of miles to the west. Per Hansa's community and kingdom are once more secure.

In *The Thresher* recourse to the law is unheard of, except in the cases of questionable paternity of illegitimate children, and then it proves ineffective. Even when the Tetzell crew burns Johnny Black's threshing rig, no hint of going to the law is ever mentioned. Johnny Black is vengefully furious, but ruthlessly practical. He buys another threshing rig immediately, "one as big as the Golden Bird," and tells his crews to keep threshing, that "sweat and profanity were the better part of their valor—for him, the more lucrative part" (pp. 418-19). He waits for a spell of rainy weather that halts all threshing, and then he beats Bory and Lornas Tetzell to a pulp as his several crews break heads and bones of the Tetzell crew in a brawl in the Mary's Hill saloon.

The most specific example revealing Per Hansa's will to power and position is the direct challenge to his leadership. Torkel Tallaksen, the rich newcomer from Minnesota who has already made one fortune in the new world, plays a very small role in *Giants* but a crucial one dramatizing the theme of power and kingship. Per Hansa has always done everything bigger, better, or first. Now, however, Tallaksen plans to build the first frame house on the prairie, and comes to hire Per Hansa and others to haul lumber for the new house from Worthington, Minnesota, ninety miles away.

"Are you going to build?" Per Hansa asked, quietly.

"You bet I am. Isn't that what I've been telling you? . . . there's a lot to do before I get everything ready; but I intend to hire plenty of help and get it done in a jiffy. See? I've come out here to *break prairie*, I want you to know. . . . I don't see any nameable reason why a smart man couldn't farm a whole section of land like this—or even more" (pp. 301-2, Rølvaag's emphasis, my ellipsis).

Tallaksen is a loud, swaggering braggart, and the reader cannot like him, but Tallaksen too has all those "positive" American frontier qualities: ambition, energy, impatience, recklessness, and optimism. His offer to pay Per Hansa in "work or cash—but I prefer cash, for then it's over with," although crude and condescending, should not normally excite the anger in a neighbor that it does in Per Hansa.

His reply to Tallaksen's request leaves no doubt that Per Hansa envies Tallaksen's power and position; Per Hansa recognizes that here is a rival prince to challenge his kingdom:

> If you would take the money that you intend to spend in building and put it into cattle and horses and machinery, and hire help enough to run them, then the devil himself couldn't keep up with you. In a few years *you'd be king of all of us*—though God knows we'd much rather have another. But this I tell you. . . . if you start from the other end and do as you've been proposing, then you and I will fight—yes, you and I! *for both the scepter and the crown*" (p. 302, my emphasis).

Per Hansa refuses to help Tallaksen haul lumber and "without another word he sprang up from the chest and left the house." He calls the oxen in a "gruff voice": "that day he kept on breaking as long as he could see" (p. 304). Per Hansa's precipitous and compensatory action, particularly in the light of Tallaksen's comment, "I've come out here to *break prairie*, I want you to know," clearly indicates the similarity of the desires and goals of the two men, as well as commenting on the intensity of Per Hansa's ambitions. Per Hansa has joyful exuberance and Tallakesen no humour at all, but underneath these obvious differences, their ambitions for wealth and power are essentially the same. Both are typical products—archetypes—of the American frontier. In the years to come Per Hansa realizes his fairy tale kingdom, described by Tonseten in the same material terms that Tallaksen states "a smart man" ought to be able to accomplish "out here." Tonseten reports to the newly arrived minister to the settlement: "Per Hansa—that is to say, Per Holm—he has got rich out here. . . . He is now settled on three quarters of land" (p. 356, my ellipsis).

Per Hansa in *Giants* and Johnny Black in *The Thresher* achieve their material goals. But Rølvaag and Krause, fascinated with the potential dangers and evils of rugged individualism, are "preoccupied with the human cost of empire building."[6] The similarity between Beret, wife to

Per Hansa, and Lilice, wife to Johnny Black, is at points so close that Rølvaag's characterization of Beret almost appears to have been an influence on Krause's creation of Lilice. Beret and Lilice can not share Per Hansa's and Johnny Black's dream of America as another name for opportunity. Beret and Lilice recognize that their husbands' energy, ambition, optimism, conquests, and pride contain the elements of destruction. Both women visualize an oncoming and inevitable catastrophe, a far different reality fostered by the frontier from that described by Turner, and one which far outweighs their husbands' desires of acquisition and power. Rather than sharing in the joys of triumph and subjugation, Beret and Lilice cringe at the hardening ruthlessness accompanying the conquest. When Per Hansa finally tells his neighbors how he removed the Irish landmarks, "he made it sound exactly like a fairy tale" (p. 140). But Beret examines her husband closely: "Was this the person in whom she had believed no evil could dwell? . . . Had it always been thus with him? [. . . .] The explanation was plain; this desolation out here called forth all that was evil in human nature" (p. 148, my ellipsis in brackets). Lilice, fully as fearful as Beret echoes a similar lament: "All you think of, all you live for, is machines" (p. 264).

Beret is a Christian and Lilice is a humanist.[7] To Beret Per Hansa has gained his material kingdom, but lost his soul: "You know what our life has been: land and houses, and then more land, and cattle! . . . Can't you understand that a human being ever becomes concerned over his sins and wants to be freed from them" (p. 442, my ellipsis). Lilice sees all of the best human qualities of kindness, concern, and forgiveness suppressed in Johnny Black's desire to conquer: " 'If you'd think of us here!' she moaned. He wouldn't listen. . . . his purpose as unshaken as a rock, he went his way" (p. 420). Both wives repeat the biblical injunction: "It is terrible to fall into the hands of the living God" (*Giants*, p. 433; *The Thresher*, p. 346). Both wives drift in and out of insanity, their vision of foreboding tragedy becoming more and more real. Even their images of destruction are similar. For Beret the prairie itself becomes an evil troll that will devour them all: "now she could see the monster clearer. The face was unmistakable! . . . The eyes—deep, dark caves in the cloud—were closed. . . . Black and lean the whole face, but of such gigantic, menacing proportions! . . . And the terrible creature was spreading everywhere" (p. 321, my ellipsis). In her increasing derangement Lilice visualizes the threshing machine, animated and malicious, as "a monster with open jaws to swallow all she loved"[8] (p. 417).

The final image in each novel fulfills the fearful reality of Beret's and Lilice's vision. In *Giants* "The Great Plain Drinks the Blood of Christian Men and Is Satisfied"; Per Hansa dies in the snowstorm, his stiffened and decaying corpse discovered beside a haystack, his back to the mouldering hay: "his face was ashen and drawn. His eyes were set toward the west" (p. 453). Johnny Black in "The Season of Grain in the Harvest" dies in a threshing fire:

> From the engine came the hiss of steam; from the separator a dull crackling. But Johnny lay as if earth were a good shoulder on which to rest. A knee was a little crooked. Then they saw that one fist was clenched tight. When they pried it open, a scattering of wheat, golden, unseared by flame, rolled over the callused flesh and fell to the ground (p. 488).

The catastrophe seems complete; yet the concluding images in both novels are compellingly ambiguous and paradoxical. On the one hand, the reader can find hope in the final images: Per Hansa even in death looks toward the West and the promise of the future; Johnny Black clutches the hard harvested kernels that fall to earth in the cycle of life's renewal. On the other hand, both final images can be seen to contain no hope at all: Per Hansa's frozen corpse looks forward to an America of unfulfilled promise and shattered hopes; Johnny Black even in death does not willingly relinquish his grasp upon the wheat, and symbolically his material ambitions and power.[9]

Hope for or redemption in the future is hard to recognize from either author's subsequent writings. Rølvaag published three novels: *Pure Gold, Peder Victorious,* and *Their Fathers' God*. All three finally end in tragedy.[10] Rølvaag's artistic conscience does not allow him to deny the truth of his characters and his tragic vision of America. Herbert Krause wrote another unpublished novel about the German-American "pockerbrush" community he immortalized in *Wind Without Rain* and *The Thresher.* This untitled novel was the story of a World War II veteran returning to the "pockerbrush" community with a Japanese war-bride and the attendant problems of alienation and acceptance. This novel too ended in tragedy. Herbert Krause burned the manuscript shortly after its completion in the late 1940's.[11] *The Oxcart Trail,* published in 1954, is really an unfinished historical romance and an enigma, for it raises the question: Why did Herbert Krause apparently reject, ignore or at the very least turn away from his "pockerbrush" subject completely? Historically fascinating, *The Oxcart Trail* is structurally faulty and thematically uncertain and does not have the power, however dark that power might be, of his two earlier novels.[12] *The Thresher* is Herbert Krause's greatest artistic success with its powerful characterization of the thresher, Johnny Black, and its dark and tragic vision of the Turner thesis and frontier-formed American character.

Notes

1. Frederick Jackson Turner, *The Frontier in American History* (New York: Holt, 1920), p. 32. See also Robert Steensma, "Rølvaag and Turner's Frontier Thesis," *North Dakota Quarterly*, 27 (1959), 100-104.

2. For example, the excellent, realistic description of the cradling match between Mr. Dunkel and Old Geppert is not undercut by Aunt Phrena's "Spite Match," but it is overdone when the solemn pastor repeats the injunction and adds the prophetic "Beware that you do not tempt the anger of the Lord" (p. 75). The reader knows that Gretel, Dunkel's small daughter, is asleep in the wheat and will die to conclude the first section of the novel because he has been told repeatedly several pages earlier that Gretel, asleep in the field against a shock of oats (p. 66) "crawled into the bushes again yesterday and went to sleep" (p. 67). The afternoon of the cradling match, just about nap time, Gretel disappears: "That Gretel—wonder where she's gone this time?" (p. 73). And then just as the match begins Mrs. Dunkel's frantic "Did you see Gretel anywhere? I can't find her" (p. 75) leaves absolutely no doubt that she is out there in the wheat to be cut down in the last couple rods of the match by her father's sickle, "like lightning in the grain . . . . going forward, going home, coming to the lilac bushes at the end of the piece" (p. 76). The overworked foreshadowing decreases the drama and increases the sentimentality. Snoose's bad fortune read in the milk cup topped off with his "Gramma said I never would live long," is another example of intrusively obvious foreshadowing (p. 147).

3. O. E. Rølvaag, *Giants in the Earth*, Perennial Library edition (New York: Harper, 1965), p. 103, my ellipsis.

4. Herbert Krause, *The Thresher* (New York: Bobbs-Merrill, 1946; Sioux Falls, South Dakota: Brevet Press, 1976), p. 274.

5. This impatience and lack of concern for government regulations are even more obvious in the Irish settlers who have staked the land but have not registered their claims. However, "justice" is not all on the side of the Norwegians; as one of the Irish settlers points out: "he was a thief and a blackguard who had destroyed another man's landmarks" (p. 142). Beret echoes precisely the same view: "Where I come from it was always considered a shameful sin to destroy another man's landmarks."

6. Lincoln Colcord, Introduction to *Giants in the Earth*, p. xi.

7. The contrasting views of Beret's Christianity vary from seeing her as a pietistic, guilt-ridden fanatic who precipitates Per Hansa's death to viewing her as Kierkegaard's "Knight of Faith" following God's divine imperative. See Barbara Meldrum, "Fate, Sex and Naturalism in Rølvaag's Trilogy," in *Ole Rølvaag: Artist and Cultural Leader*, edited by Gerald Thorson (Northfield, Minnesota: St. Olaf College Press, 1975), pp. 41-50, particularly p. 45. See also Harold P. Simonson, "Rølvaag and Kierkegaard," *Scandinavian Studies* (Winter, 1977), pp. 67-80.

8. See also *The Thresher*, p. 420: "It's the thresher. A big red thresher, Robin; coming like a huge grasshopper . . . . coming for him and he won't listen."

9. I am indebted to Professor Marilyn Klawiter, Department of English, Augustana College, for pointing out this additional and even darker ambiguity in the final image of *The Thresher*.

10. *Peder Victorious* and *Their Fathers' God* are a single entity in the same way that *Giants in the Earth* is a single entity. *Giants in the Earth* was originally published as two books: *I de dage* (*The Landtaking*) and *Riket Grundlaegges* (*The Founding of the Kingdom*).

11. For this information I am indebted to Professor S. G. Froiland, Director, Center for Western Studies, Augustana College, Sioux Falls, South Dakota.

12. Herbert Krause's friends at Augustana College agreed that Krause had felt pressured to finish the novel in a hurry and that he thought it had been published too soon.

Giants in the Earth as Saga

NEIL T. ECKSTEIN

Neil T. Eckstein, associate professor of English at the University of Wisconsin, Oshkosh, has written on bicultural writing for Ole Rølvaag: Artist and Cultural Leader (*1975*).

The term "saga," like "epic," is subject to a certain inflation or dilution of meaning. Not only do we have John Galsworthy's *Forsythe Saga*, but also, when a local booster group in Gopher Prairie, Minnesota, publishes a twenty-four page collection of pictures and captions about the old hometown, it is entitled pompously—"The Saga of Gopher Prairie." When the first English edition of Ole E. Rølvaag's *Giants in the Earth* appeared in 1927, it was subtitled, *A Saga of the Prairie*. In later editions, the subtitle was dropped. But with or without the subtitle, Rølvaag's novel has a special affinity to the saga tradition, and, with some justification, may be called a "saga" in the broader and modern sense of the term. As the Rølvaag biographers state it:

> If an estimate were to be made concerning what literary influences are most apparent in the epic of Per Hansa and his wife, it would have to include Ibsen, the Old Norse Sagas, the Norwegian fairy tales, and the Nordland dialect and folk memories.[1]

Literary "influence" is at best a nebulous term because writers, as observant and sensitive persons, are "influenced" in one way or another by an exceedingly wide range of experiences. Yet certain writers may stand indebted in an unusual degree to a particular literary tradition. In the case of Rølvaag, the debt to all Scandinavian literature, and, in particular, to those strands identified above, can be assumed. In short, Rølvaag's debt to the saga tradition can be singled out, described, and assessed with a fair degree of accuracy.

We must recall that Rølvaag was by profession a teacher of Norwegian language and literature. When he was a graduate student at the University in Christiania (Oslo) in 1905-1906, he came directly under the tutelage of Professors Gerhard Gran and Ernst Sars, both recognized as scholars of high repute and both fervently committed to a deeply nationalistic point of view. It must be recalled that it was in 1905 that Norway severed the last ties of dependence with Sweden, and acquired her own king. There was, in the historical and literary scholarship of the period, led by Gran, Sars, and others, an assertive claim that Old Norse literature, whether written in Iceland or Norway, was uniquely and distinctively the cultural property of those two nations, and was not pan-Scandinavian. To this Rølvaag assented heartily, and supported this view during his whole career.[2]

Furthermore, Rølvaag could hardly have avoided a strong and continuous exposure to the Old Norse sagas; they were among the most important manifestations of the "faedrearv" (heritage from the fathers) and a good deal of Rølvaag's career was devoted to making his fellow Norwegian-Americans appreciative of their remarkable heritage.

In a little notebook entry extant in the Rølvaag papers, dating from 1922, or perhaps earlier, Rølvaag put down the germ of his thought on the story that was about to emerge as *I de dage*, the first half of what we recognize as *Giants in the Earth*:

Da praerien var ung
Landnám
Hoved karakteren: Hans Olsa og Per Persa.
Petrina. Gurina.
Barn: Ole, Jens, (Kari) Jørgina.[3]

(When the prairie was young
The Land-Taking
Chief Characters: Hans Olsa and Per Persa.
Petrina. Gurina.
Children: Ole, Jens (Kari) Jorgina.)

The most interesting item to note is the early inclusion of the Old Norse or Icelandic term, *landnám*. The term was retained as a subtitle for the Norwegian edition of *I de dage* in 1924, and appears in the English editions (translated as "The Land-Taking") as the title for Book I of *Giants in the Earth.*

Landnámabok was, of course, one of the earliest of the Icelandic sagas, recording in meticulous and almost endless detail the settlement of Iceland by Viking colonists shortly after its discovery in 874 A.D. Some four thousand of these colonizers and their descendants are mentioned by name, giving the Icelandic people a vivid sense of their roots. Rølvaag's use of *landnám* suggests that he saw a remarkably parallel phenomenon occurring on the Minnesota and Dakota prairies, almost exactly one millenium later. Like the Iceland of a thousand years ago, the prairie lands of our North American Great Plains were bleak and nearly uninhabited, at least by European standards. To the near-empty land came the land-takers, out on the very rim of civilization, cut off by great distances from their Motherland, and forced to live in primitive isolation.

In *Egil's Saga* there are some passages which capture this moment of entry upon the new and empty land:

> Skallagrím came to land where a big headland ran out into the sea, and beyond the headland a narrow isthmus. They carried their cargo ashore there, calling the place Knarrarnes. Next Skallagrím explored the countryside: There was a lot of marshland there and spacious forest, with plenty of room between mountains and sea, ample seal-hunting and good fishing. . . . Then Skallagrím took land in settlement between mountains and sea. . . . Here he established house and home, calling it Borg and the firth Borgarfjørd; and the countryside inland from there, that too they named after the firth.[4]

Although the vast Minnesota and Dakota prairies were far from either sea or mountains, there is a strikingly nautical tone to Per Hansa's journey across the trackless and undulating prairie. But he finally caught up with the others. Soon Per Hansa, like Skallagrím, turned his attention to "land-taking":

> "How about it, you fellows?" . . . "I suppose there's a little more land left around here, isn't there, after you've got through?"
>
> "*Land*? Good God! Per Hansa, what are you talking about? Take whatever you please, from here to the Pacific Ocean!" Tønseten's enthusiasm got so far away with him that he had to pull one of his hands out of his waistband and make a sweeping circle with it in the air.
>
> "You must take a look around as soon as you can," Hans Olsa said, "and see if you find anything better that meets your fancy. In the meanwhile I've put down a stake for you on the quarter section that lies north of mine. We'll go over and have a look at it pretty soon. Sam Solum wanted it, but I told him he'd better leave it till you came . . . . You see, you would be next to the creek there; and then you and I would be the nearest neighbours, just as we've always planned.[5]

Per Hansa threw himself into the enterprise of land-taking with gusto, out-pacing the others from the beginning. Dreaming of a "kingdom" that he could rule like a petty Icelandic chieftain or *godi*, he would have understood Skallagrím perfectly. The saga states simply, "Skallagrím was a great man for work," and then proceeds to give us some idea of the scale of his land-taking enterprise.[6] Per Hansa, too, was "a great man for work!"

Beyond the "land-taking" motif, there are a number of additional thematic parallels that link *Giants in the Earth* to the saga tradition. The most pervasive of these is the belief in Destiny or Fate. If, as Peter Hallbert asserts, "Fatalism is one of the essential elements in the world of the Icelandic saga,"[7] then *Giants in the Earth* does not lack for this essential. Again and again "Fate," "Providence," and "Destiny" are alluded to, not only by Beret in her brooding pessimism, but by other characters as well. When Tønseten had been successful in persuading twenty Norwegians to settle as neighbors, he reflected smugly that "Destiny had used him as her tool" (p. 164). When Sørine informed Per Hansa that his child had been born with the caul, she implied, as a footnote explains, that the child had been singled out by Destiny for something extraordinary (p. 240). In yet another episode, the husband of the deranged woman explained the death of their son: "I can't tell how it happened! Fate just willed it so. Such things are not to be explained" (p. 320). Even the ebullient Per Hansa could be pressed to the point of acknowledging the role of fate in his life. When, in the midst of the blinding blizzard, it seemed he was about to perish, he thought, "A strange fate, this, I'll be damned if it isn't!" (p. 272).

But if fate is acknowledged by nearly all the others in the story, it is with Beret a brooding obsession. Mingled with morbid religious guilts and deep psychological fears, Beret's sense of destiny exceeds the objective framework of fate in the saga tradition. When, for example, Gísli learned some bad news upon his return to Iceland, he merely responded, "That is the way it must be," in an attitude of calm acceptance (Hallberg, p. 94). Beret, on the other hand, was incapable of that kind of objectivity and terseness.

It is, then, a matter of honor to submit to one's fate without whimpering, as Hallberg explains:

> It is by his attitude toward his fate more than in any other way that a saga character can prove his mettle. He can succumb to his fate, broken and resigned, or he can meet it unbroken and with heroic affirmation. Here is where he reveals his worth as a man and establishes his own renown: the judgment by posterity of a dead man (p. 88).

Nowhere in *Giants in the Earth* is this submission with honor stronger than in the final journey of Per Hansa. Although, as a rational man he protests against the folly of this journey ("Do you want to drive me out into the jaws of death?" p. 454), he finally resolves that he must undertake the journey, and he shoves off on his skis with an "Oh, well—here goes! . . ." (p. 463).

To be sure, Per Hansa is no Viking warrior, challenging his opponent to the *holmgang* at the slightest breach of honor; he is a pragmatic man who, in true Yankee fashion, keeps his eye on the main chance. Yet, on his own terms, he is a man of honor. Like a saga hero, he honors a pact of sworn brotherhood with Hans Olsa, and it is this point of honor rather than the nagging of Beret that drives him forth on his last and fatal quest. Yet, Per Hansa is capable, like many of the saga heroes, of cunning and even deceitfulness in protecting the interests and honor of his friends. By destroying the landstakes of the Irish claimants, Per Hansa acts out of loyalty to his friends, especially to Hans Olsa. As Hallberg concludes, "to use cunning or guile against an enemy was not regarded as disgraceful for a warrior or hero" (p. 107).

Nearly as pervasive in the sagas as the theme of accepting one's fate with honor is the parallel theme of revenge or conflict. If one's honor is compromised, it must be avenged, either by lawful resolution or by resorting to bloodshed and violence. In fact, it is this endless round of avenging murders and the subsequent negotiations for settlement by the paying of *wergelt* that strikes the modern reader as the most characteristic feature of the saga. Obviously, in telling the "Saga of the Prairie," Rølvaag did not wish to make of his hero some kind of Western gun-slinger, with notches in his gun handle to account for lawless slayings. Of this kind of Western hero we have had an abundance in our sub-literature and in the legends of our oral tradition.

The only "battle" scene of the story is the brawl which broke out with the Irish over the conflicting land claims. This episode, a kind of saga within the novel, is told with the same terse vividness and directness that we find so frequently in the old sagas:

> When Hans Olsa saw the Irishman loom up before him in that threatening attitude, he stared at him blankly, and stood for a moment as if rooted to the ground. Then, all of a sudden, the upper part of his body seemed to stretch; he stepped aside to evade the onslaught . . . his left fist shot out and struck the man below the ear. There was a crashing sound; with a loud groan the man sank in a heap and lay perfectly still (p. 147).

The brawl was over soon enough, and, unlike most of the saga battles, the "casualties" turned out to be minor bruises. Hans Olsa emerges as the hero of the brawl, and, with some persistence and cunning, Per Hansa is able to bring about a reconciliation with the Irish adversaries. Perhaps in the very choice of Irishmen as adversaries, Rølvaag was consciously reflecting the saga tradition which tells of many a Norse and Irish confrontation in those old times.

There is, however, a deeper and more pervasive conflict in the novel than the brawl over the land claims. But the enemy in this conflict is no human adversary. As the English title suggests, there were "giants" to contend with, and, in spite of the opinion of some Rølvaag scholars that the "giants" are the heroic protagonists, the pioneers themselves, the majority view is that the "giants" of the novel are those elusive and unnamed forces within the prairie itself that contend in bitter conflict with the pioneers.[8] In other words, in order to establish the tension and conflict of the novel, Rølvaag endows the forces of nature with malevolence and cruelty, at least in the minds of the pioneers. In so doing, he draws upon the vast and intriguing world of Norse folklore and myth, populating the prairie with trolls and archtrolls and evil spirits. In order to achieve this Rølvaag gives us extensive passages of nature description, a device noted by Hallberg as almost completely lacking in the old sagas (p. 71). By personifying nature, Rølvaag reaches back into Old Norse mythology in the times before the sagas, and into Norse folklore in the times after the sagas.

But not all of the conflicts of the novel are transposed or externalized. The most profound conflicts are internal ones, penetrating deeply into the psychological make-up of the chief characters. In this respect, Rølvaag shows his debt to Ibsen and other modern writers more than to the old sagas, which usually treated conflict in external and objective terms.

There are a few places in the novel, however, where the very style of saga directness and objectivity breaks through as a kind of sub-stratum in a multi-layered literary complexity. The first paragraph of the last chapter, "The Great Plains Drinks the Blood of Christian Men and Is Satisfied," is strikingly saga-like in its rhetoric:

> Many and incredible are the tales the grandfathers tell from those days when the wildnerness was yet untamed, and when they, unwittingly, founded the Kingdom. There was the Red Son of the Great Prairie, who hated the Palefaces with a hot hatred; stealthily he swooped down upon them, tore up and laid waste the little settlements. Great was the terror he spread; bloody the saga concerning him (p. 424).

Gudrun Hovde Gvaale contends that there are a number of stylistic reflections of the sagas in Rølvaag's novel. She notes the repitition of many old adages and aphorisms; the lively dialogue, brought closer to the saga tradition by Rølvaag's use of the dialect of his native Nordland; the use of folk superstitions, etc.[9] We must, however, recall that Gvaale is discussing the original Norwegian novel and reading it with a native's sensitivity to the nuances of language and idiom. Yet, even if we limit our comparisons to the English translation of the novel and to good English translations of the sagas, we can establish some sense of stylistic continuity, at least in isolated passages.

It is, however, in the creation and delineation of character in relation to setting that Rølvaag often seems closest to the tap-roots of the old sagas. As W. P. Ker pointed out, "In the material conditions of Icelandic life in the 'Saga Age' there was all the stuff that was required for heroic narrative."[10] Unlike more "civilized" parts of Christendom that were turning more and more to high romance, the Icelanders of the twelfth and thirteenth centuries lived in a primitive and impoverished manner. It is, nevertheless, this very meanness of external circumstances that thrusts the Icelandic saga into a greater grasp with reality. There are no damsels in distress, no dragons to slay, no castles with troubadours and tapestries—there is only a stark and bleak world of external reality, and upon this sparse stage the heroic dimensions of the chief protagonists stand forth boldly and uncluttered. It is so also in Rølvaag's novel. As Gvaale has noted, the pioneer society on the prairie bears a striking resemblance to that of Iceland—right down to the sod houses.[11] Per Hansa, like Skalla-grim or Egil, like Gunnar or Njál, stands out as a leader among his peers, not because of inherited status or refinement of manners, but because of innate ability and cleverness. Even though Beret is cast less in the saga mold, it is through Beret's anguish that we often are made aware of the sharp contrasts between natural (or pagan) values and Christian values—a theme that a number of the sagas uncover as an underlying and pervasive source of tension and conflict. Although Beret is developed in a very different way from Hallgjerd in *Njál's Saga*, like Hallgjerd, Beret is a perpetrator of conflict, and her man falls victim in the process. Even the somewhat ludicrous Tønseten would not be out of place in an old saga, for there is also room for comic contrast, and Tønseten's "bear" that turned out to be a badger would have amused the old Icelanders greatly. And it was, we recall, Tønseten who stayed in bed until late afternoon, trembling with cowardice and fear, on the day after the brawl with the Irish (p. 152). The Icelanders would have roared uncontrollably over that one!

The debt of Rølvaag to the saga tradition is an enormous one, and many of the finest touches in the novel seem to suggest some echoes of those old sagas. Rølvaag has exposed his American readers to a whole new literary world, and we are enriched by this exposure. Of course, *Giants in the Earth* is more than "saga" in a derivative sense; it is a genuinely creative work which incorporates, in a masterful way, many strands of a rich literary past into a coherent whole.

Notes

1. Theodore Jorgenson and Nora Solum, *Ole Edvart Rølvaag: A Biography* (New York: Harper, 1939), p. 344.

2. Jorgenson and Solum, p. 93.

3. Rølvaag Papers (Norwegian-American Historical Association, Northfield, Minnesota), Box 25.

4. *Egil's Saga*, tr. Gwyn Jones (New York: The American Scandinavian Foundation and Twayne, 1960), pp. 79-80.

5. O. E. Rølvaag, *Giants in the Earth*, Harper's Modern Classics Edition (New York: Harper, 1929), pp. 29-30.

6. *Egil's Saga*, p. 81.

7. Peter Hallberg, *The Icelandic Saga*, tr. Paul Schach (Lincoln: Univ. of Nebraska Press, 1962), p. 87.

8. Among the Rølvaag scholars expounding the first view is Einar Haugen: see "O. E. Rølvaag: The Man in His Work," *Ole Rølvaag: Artist and Cultural Leader*, ed. Gerald Thorson (Northfield, Minnesota: St. Olaf College Press, 1975), p. 22.

9. Gudrun Hovde Gvaale, *O. E. Rølvaag: nordmann og amerikanar* (Oslo: Universitetsforlaget, 1962), p. 363.

10. William P. Ker, *Epic and Romance: Essays on Medieval Literature* (New York: Dover, 1957), p. 200.

11. Gvaale, p. 363.

Shucking the Pastoral Ideal: Sources and Meaning of Realism in Scandinavian Immigrant Fiction About the Pioneer Farm Experience

CHRISTER LENNART MOSSBERG

Christer Mossberg, who teaches in the Honors College of the University of Oregon, is preparing a monograph on Scandinavian immigrant writers for the Western Writers Series.

The metaphors and image clusters associated with the American West have been analyzed by many notable literary critics and historians; Henry Nash Smith's *Virgin Land* (Cambridge: Harvard, 1950) and Leo Marx's *The Machine in the Garden* (New York: Oxford, 1964) have been particularly influential in shaping American critical thought about the image of the West as molding the "collective representation" and the "collective imagination" of the American national character. These two works demonstrate that art is not generated in a vacuum—that there is constant interplay between the literary imagination and the social, economic, cultural, and intellectual ideas at work in a particular society. If we are to interpret American literature, then, we must understand the circumstances out of which the literature arose. Despite the massive research efforts of both Smith and Marx to place the literature in its historical context, they ignore one of the most important historical events of the nineteenth and early twentieth centuries in the conclusions they reach about the shaping forces of the American character—the mass influx of immigrants into the Old Northwest. The purpose of this paper is to establish the necessity of integrating the immigrant experience into our conception of the American imagination, and in this context, to explore the nature of three immigrant groups—the Swedes, Norwegians, and Danes—in an effort to illustrate how the immigrant fiction about the pioneer farm experience in the West challenges the popular myths of "the garden" and the "pastoral ideal."

One of the ideas governing both *Virgin Land* and *The Machine in the Garden* is that a major distinction can be drawn between "serious" art (i.e., Hawthorne, Melville, Thoreau) and sentimental art, such as the Beadle dime novels. According to Smith and Marx, what makes our "serious" writers "serious" is their awareness, either conscious or intuitive, of the gap between the rural ideals we look to for values and meaning, and the fact of industrialism which increasingly determines the shape of our society. The "serious" writers' conviction that the pastoral myth does not reflect the totality of the American experience induces an ironic view on their part towards the pastoral ideal, which they undercut in their writing. Sentimental pastoralism, on the other hand, exploits the escapism inherent in myths that are not anchored to experience, and feeds to the mass reading audience all the western adventure, romance, and violence it can absorb.

There is no such dividing line between serious and sentimental pastoralism in the immigrant fiction. That is not to say there is no sentimental immigrant literature—there certainly is, including a minor genre of wish-fulfillment novels; nor do I mean to imply that there are not different levels of artistic achievement. There obviously are, which I will be discussing. But the immigrant fiction on pioneer farming arose from the writers' personal experience of living on the land. Even in the "serious" American fiction, the reality of the frontier experience is symbolized or made into fable; but because most of the immigrant writers at one time had worked the soil, there is an air of authenticity in the fiction they write when life on the farm is described. The jobs associated with agriculture are not idealized, and common men and women perform their daily activities in a setting that is rendered in vivid detail to recreate the actual experience. A body of literature exists, then, that redefines the agrarian myth according to the experiences of immigrant farmers working the land. Most of the writers would be termed non-"serious" by Marx, yet they interpreted the complexity of the western experience for a mass audience both in this country and in Europe. I will analyze several elements inherent in the immigrant experience which kept the immigrant writers from swallowing the rhetoric of the garden and which enabled them to interpret the pioneer experience in markedly different ways than its representation in mainstream American literature. By examining accounts of early immigrant settlement in the Northwest, we can trace the process of the redefinition of the myth of "the garden," as well as gain insight into the forces shaping the immigrant literary imagination which led to the stress on realism, in the early fiction, and exploration of the immigrant psychology in the later fiction.

In 1838, *Ole Rynning's True Account of America* was published in Christiania, Norway, to provide a "trustworthy and fairly detailed account of the country" in order to dispel the "great . . . ignorance of the people" and the "false and preposterous reports [which] were believed as full truth."[1] Rynning describes his experiences in America and gives his readers this warning: "Many go to America with such unreasonable expectations and ideas that they necessarily must find themselves disappointed. The first stumbling block, ignorance of the language, is enough to dishearten many at once. *The person who neither can nor will work must never expect that riches and luxurious living will be open to him. No, in America one gets nothing without work; but it is true that by work one can expect some day to achieve better circumstances*" (p. 93). It is important to realize that the myth of what the West had to offer was available to the immigrants, and not arrived at retrospectively. In fact, Rynning refers specifically to one myth operant in Norway that "those who emigrate to America will find cultivated farms, houses, clothes, and furniture ready for them." In somewhat of an understatement, Rynning warns his readers that "this is a false supposition" (p. 75). We know that *Rynning's True Account* was read by prospective immigrants; an immigrant of 1839 says: "Hardly any other Norwegian publication has been purchased and read with such avidity as this Rynning's *Account of America*" (Blegen, p. 17). We also know that letters which arrived from America were copied and circulated from house to house, and that thousands were printed in Scandinavian newspapers. Many of these letters discuss the advantages of farm life in the American West, where the land is often described as a "real Canaan, where the abundance of nature may be called a flow of milk and honey."[2] Therefore the myth was perpetrated even after experience confronted it. But the letters also discuss the "dog years," the sixteen-hour days behind the plow, the crop yield, the rainfall, the bushels per acre. Thus we hear two voices speaking in the letters: one is abstract and idealized, drawing its images and allusions from the Bible and Pontoppidan. That the language of this voice is similar to the language describing the myth of the garden shows the kind of rhetoric available to the writer who wants to romanticize or idealize the subject. This voice in the letters often expresses a wish-fulfillment, or in its most concrete form, a projection of an anticipated future. The other voice expresses the perception of the farmer. That voice is practical, analytical, and informative. It draws its descriptive power from a working experience on the land and it shows a consciousness of historical change affecting both the land and the immigrant group as the Northwest is pioneered and settled. It is this simple, practical voice that informs the early literary efforts of the immigrant writers: this voice cares about gingham and calico, axes, sod turf, and dugouts; when to plant crops, how long the growing season is, what "pie" is like; we hear about strange black funnels in the sky, statistics on bushels per acre, and lack of rainfall on the plains.

As can be seen, much of the early immigrant fiction is little more than a fictionalized diary. In fact, many authors intrude on the narrative to tell the reader that they are recording actual observations, events, or experiences. There is little attempt at characterization, or even at structuring a plot. The purpose of the fiction is to describe the land and the different stages in the immigrant group's adjustment to living on the prairies. As a body of literature, the fiction is first telling, then re-telling, the same essential story which more or less follows this sequence: the reasons for leaving Scandinavia; the journey across the Atlantic and the problems encountered before reaching the land they settle on; the hardships of breaking the prairie sod and establishing a productive farm; the development of the farm and of religious, political, and social institutions of infant communities; the rising tension between Scandinavian and American values, most commonly expressed through the experiences of immigrant children in the American common schools. In the major fiction written in the 1920's and 1930's, another dominant theme is added to the story: alienation experienced by the second and third generations as they grapple for meaningful values.

For the Scandinavian-American community and for the large audience of prospective immigrants in Scandinavia, the early immigrant fiction served a practical function. More a document than anything else, it tells the readers what to expect when they reach the Northwest and gives them possible ways to respond to the new environment. The literature recreates situations that were common to the group experience, and thereby provides invaluable practical and psychological support for the immigrants in that their own experience was anticipated, reinforced, and validated. On a psychological level, the literature also helped to endow the immigrant group with its own distinct cultural identity. To have their experiences recorded emphasized the collective past of the immigrant group, and made the immigrants feel that there was a permanence to what they were doing in the West. It gave them a sense that they had taken part in, and created, history.

The literature also expresses the desires of the immigrant group to elevate their own experience and confer a dignity upon their struggles and achievements. Reading the literature from this perspective, we can view it as a justification for emigration. One has to remember that in the nineteenth century, several myths circulated in Scandinavia that countered the image of the American garden. The landed ruling class and government officials, afraid that they would lose their supply of cheap labor for their farms and draftees for the military, tried to "frighten [immigrants] with terrible tales about the dreadful sea monsters, and . . . man-eating wild animals in the new world" (Blegen, p. 17). The landed classes in Scandinavia did not allow the immigrants to feel the pride and self-confidence of the "idealized frontier farmer" that Smith, for example, alludes to in *Virgin Land.* On the contrary, their opinions about the American farmer are quite different. "America is filling up with the scum of the world. There is no honor in being a farmer there."[3] But neither myths about man-eating wild animals or the criminal element in America could deter the mass outflow of peasant farmers, so the landed classes could only refer to immigration as a "bloodletting good for the nation . . . a sewer carrying away all kinds of waste."[4]

The need to disprove these myths helped to stimulate literary activity in the new world and resulted in ennobling the group experience as I have discussed above. Perhaps the two poles of operating myths about the American West—the idealized farmer in the garden on the one hand, the scum and man-eating wild animals on the other—served to cancel out each other's distortions and enabled the immigrants, particularly the immigrant writers, to perceive and to express their experiences in realistic terms.

It may seem unlikely that these immigrant farmers, extremely susceptible to the American myth of unending, fertile soil where all men lived under the same laws and enjoyed the same democratic rights, would be able to describe their experiences in realistic terms. But several factors inherent in the immigrant experience itself help to explain how and why they resisted the rhetoric of the garden. The pain and sadness the immigrants felt when leaving parents and friends immediately made them aware of a complexity of feelings: every joyous expectation had an emotional equivalent of longing or regret. Death and sickness on the ship voyage across the Atlantic made them acutely aware of their own vulnerability. Before they ever stepped on the American prairies, then, they had paid a tremendous price: their own suffering denied the simplicity of the world vision inherent in a pastoral idealization. They could feel strength from a collective identity established by shared experience without idealizing those experiences. In this way, the experience gained meaning and value without being distorted or romanticized.

The memories of the immigrants also made them skeptical of the garden rhetoric—many had experienced the underside of the pastoral ideal in Europe and had a more complex view of what constituted the farm experience than the garden myth allowed for. They had worked on large, landed estates, sometimes under brutal labor conditions, and had held the lowest rank in a rigid social and economic hierarchy. They were able to compare and evaluate their circumstances on the prairies by measuring it against their own past experiences. Their expectations of life in the American West and the criteria they used to evaluate it were informed more by a conception of farm life as they had lived it than by the rhetoric of the garden which had no ties to a real farm existence.

The immigrants' previous existence in Europe, then, had a crucial impact on their interpretation of the American experience. Contrary to the Adamic myth where Americans saw themselves at the dawn of a new history, cut off from Old World institutions and links with the past, the farmers who actually settled the West brought their European institutions with them. The religious, social, and cultural institutions on the prairies in the last half of the nineteenth century were just as much transplanted from Europe as they were shaped by circumstances in the American West. In the first big wave of emigration from Scandinavia, the peasant farmers usually came in groups from the same parish and then settled together in a virgin area of the Northwest. These small outposts attracted later emigrants, as this letter from an early Swedish settler illustrates: "within five years my father's parents, my grandmother, . . . all the sisters and brothers of my father and of my mother and many other relatives of ours had arrived in Minnesota. . . . In our community . . . most of the people probably belonged to our family, and nearly all of them had come from the same district in Sweden. They had so completely transplanted part of Sweden to America that names of groves and homesteads were for a great part identical with those of the old country. This great emigration had been started through some personal letters" (Nelson, p. 218). In the immigrant letters, such as the one above, and in the world of the immigrant fiction, the stamp of the Old World is everywhere present. The fiction is structured by the attempt to incorporate and adapt Old World institutions to New World conditions. The immigrants readily embraced the concepts of democracy, equality, and independence associated with life as frontier farmers, but the geographical fact of the vast open spaces which gives rise to the political and social concepts of the myth also served as a threat to a people with a tradition and culture to maintain. One must consider the complexity and interplay of a two-world perspective when trying to interpret the immigrant's experience in the West. In both the letters and the fiction we discover that the wealth of possibilities offered by the American West is always associated with a sense of loss or longing for emotional, psychological, or social ties in the Old World. The notion of the garden as a new beginning, completely divorced from history, could never be accepted by the immigrants.

I have pointed out that much of the early immigrant literature is more documentary in nature than fiction. There is very little inspired creativity; the narrative voice lacks an imaginative, or literary, use of language, and there are few invented situations. But this fidelity to historical fact kept the body of immigrant fiction on the pioneer experience from drifting into the romances and adventure stories that dominate American literature for the mass market of that period.[5] The minor immigrant fiction, therefore, together with the "America letters," diaries, and journals, constitute an immigrant literary "tradition" which later writers like Ole Rølvaag, Sophus Winther, and Simon Johnson could invest with imagination to create real "art." Thus writers of the 1920's and 30's relate the story of the immigrant through the psychology of individual characterization as opposed to a simple narration of the external changes in personal lives and social communities. They were able to re-create situations which were pivotal to the group experience, allowing us as readers to share in the destinies of individual characters and thereby gain insight into what it *feels* like to be an immigrant working the soil of the American West.

The following passages illustrate how a factual event recorded in a letter is transformed by an artist, and how a "tradition" of documented events can be selected and invested with a significance and meaning that is central to the group experience. The description that follows is from a letter written by an early settler (Nelson, p. 267):

> The ground and the road and everything was soon covered several inches deep by the hoppers and on inclines, where we would go a little faster, they could not get away quick enough and were crushed by the wheels to such an extent that it made it muddy so the wheels slid sideways if the ground sloped ever so little.
>
> Numberless scissorlike mouths were gnawing on stubs of corn stalks near the roadside, the tassel was gone, the edges of the leaves were eaten away, and lines of hungry insects could be seen clinging to the center rib of the blades gnawing and cutting at the remaining inch of the stem.

The writer of this letter has a keen eye and succeeds in communicating what he sees because his description is so graphic: for example, we know how many grasshoppers there are because the road is "muddy" with them and the wheels "slid sideways." But although there is a wealth of descriptive factual information in this letter, there is nothing that tells us how men and women responded to this catastrophe. When Rølvaag describes the same event in *Giants in the Earth*, it is given a larger metaphoric meaning to represent the conflict of Old and New World values which is the crux of the immigrant experience. In the scene in *Giants*, the farmers are harvesting Per Hansa's fields just before the grasshoppers descend. Syvert's conversation makes it clear that Rølvaag is setting up the pastoral ideal of the garden: "Well, boys, in my opinion the Land of Canaan didn't have much on this country—no, I'm damned if it had! Do you suppose the children of Israel ever smelt a westerly breeze like this? Why, folks, it's blowing honey!"[6] But the garden myth is quickly undercut as swarms of grasshoppers devour the ripening wheat. Syvert associates the disaster with seven plagues that fell on Egypt "because the people *hardened themselves*," a case of typology which imposes a universal structure on the event. The disaster is interpreted as God's punishment, which gives insight into the workings of the immigrant psychology. They feel the need to be punished because they are guilt-ridden for tearing so many Old World bonds in order to settle on the American West. They feel they have betrayed their parents, their country, and their God. The effect of this guilt is seen as Beret is driven insane by the plague which she interprets as a symbol of deserved destruction. She cannot survive life on the "wild" prairie without the support of a social life based on ties to the old church and school. In the structure Rølvaag has superimposed on this event, Beret is representative of those sensibilities in the make-up of the immigrant who needs and establishes cultural and social institutions linked to the Old World. Per Hansa, on the other hand, embodies another aspect of immigrant psychology: the aggressive, hard-working vitality of the New World, the pioneer spirit that is future-oriented, productive, and courageous enough to defy grasshoppers—or even God—by firing his musket into the midst of the "devils" to save his crops. Rølvaag employs the grasshopper scene, then, to reveal the complexity, and interplay, of the thoughts and emotions which comprise the world outlook of the immigrants. Writing in the 1920's, Rølvaag is able to see the event of the grasshoppers recorded by the first generation immigrant letter writer in its larger historical context. This historical perspective allows him to juxtapose the pastoral ideal and natural disaster in order to bring irony to bear on the idealization of the garden. The scene becomes a symbolic rendering of a sociological understanding of an historical event, and in this way, art makes meaning out of history.

Thirty years ago, T. C. Blegen called the immigrant letters the "literature of the unlettered" and stressed the importance for historical study of everyday events in the lives of common men and women.[7] Much research has been done in the area of immigration study since then, especially in the last ten years in Sweden and Norway. But very little research has been done on the immigrant literature, with the exception of Dorothy Burton Skårdal's use of literary sources to write a history of the Scandinavian immigrant experience.[8] What is needed is more critical literary analysis and interpretation of the feelings, aspirations, and disappointments of the various immigrant groups as expressed in the fiction they wrote about the settling the American West. If, as Americans, we are to understand the West both as a symbol of our dreams and as an historical place settled and developed by millions of common men and women, we need to use our translating skills and make the literature of the immigrant groups accessible to the modern American reader. After all, half of the men and women who pioneered and settled the West were immigrants. Any account that attempts to show the impact of the West on the national consciousness, whether it claims to trace the American literary imagination or the American pastoral ideal, must consider the immigrant voice.

Notes

1. *Ole Rynning's True Account of America*, trans. and ed. Theodore C. Blegen (Minneapolis: The Norwegian-American Historical Association, 1926), pp. 63. In the text this work is cited as "Rynning" and its introduction as "Blegen."

2. Helge Nelson, *The Swedes and the Swedish Settlement in North America* (Lund: CWK Gleerup, 1943), p. 250.

3. James A. Peterson, *Solstad: The Old and the New* (Minneapolis: Augsburg Publishing House, 1923), p. 125.

4. John I. Kolehmainen, *The Finns in America* (New York: Teachers College Press, 1968), p. 6. There was truth in the assertion that America was filling up with "undesirables," for criminals and paupers were sent to the U.S. (Cf. Christian Hvidt, *Flight to America: The Social Background of 300,000 Danish Emigrants* (New York: Academic Press, 1975), pp. 20-23). But just as not all immigrants (guilty as they felt) were criminals, not all people shared the opinion that "bloodletting was good for the nation." In fact, the image of "bloodletting" most often was used by officials and writers in Scandinavia to refer to a draining of the countries' youth and vitality (Cf. Franklin D. Scott, "Sweden's Constructive Opposition to Emigration," *Journal of Modern History*, XXXVII (1965), pp. 307-35).

5. We do see several romances written by immigrants, most often as wish-fulfillment fantasies, but even in these novels the job of farming is generally described in realistic terms. The protagonists in these novels might, for example, in some miraculous way make a fortune from mining gold in California, but the time they spend on the prairies doing farm work is usually described in realistic detail.

6. Ole Rølvaag, *Giants in the Earth* (New York: Harper & Row, 1927), p. 340.

7. Theodore C. Blegen, *Grass Roots History* (Minneapolis: Univ. of Minnesota Press, 1947), pp. 14-27.

8. Dorothy Burton Skårdal, *The Divided Heart* (Oslo: Universitetsforlaget and Lincoln: Univ. of Nebraska Press, 1974).

Hamlin Garland's Indians and the Quality of Civilized Life

JACK L. DAVIS

Jack L. Davis is associate professor of American Studies at the University of Idaho. He has published articles on native American literature in Western American Literature *and in the* South Dakota Review, *and has an essay on W. G. Simms in* The Westering Experience in American Literature *(1977).*

Hamlin Garland's reputation today is fairly secure as a chronicler of Euro-American civilization establishing itself in the northern Midwest. In the early and latter phases of his fiction, as Donald Pizer, Jay Martin, and Robert Gish have noted,[1] Garland attacked the myth of the easy, good life in the old Northwest and introduced Eastern readers to the arduous physical and social realities on the raw middle border. *Main-Travelled Roads* (1891) and *Rose of Dutcher's Coolly* (1895) are the best known examples of that early realistic fiction. Yet in his middle phase of over two decades, beginning in 1895, Garland turned his attention farther west, apparently discarding everything he had previously said about the need for literature to deal with the unpleasant as well as the pleasant aspects of life.[2] As a consequence, most of his work during this middle period is viewed as a temporary abdication of Garland's undisputed gift for delineating the hard realities of western life.

However, Robert Gish has recently suggested that this very phase, when Garland betook himself farther west to meet ranchers, miners, Indian agents, and sundry tribes of native Americans, is the most interesting to contemporary students of western literature (Gish, p. 6). It is true that most of the dozen novels and many stories of this Far West period simply invoke the romanticized vision of the West Garland strove so hard to puncture earlier. Yet the Indian material, the stories written mainly between 1895 and 1905 but later collected in *The Book of the American Indian* (1923) and also the novel *The Captain of the Gray-Horse Troop* (1902) are truly landmark treatments of Indians. They suggest that Garland was not simply escaping back into the mythology of ideal life in the West, but actually was extending the trenchant criticism begun in his early work.

During his travels in the Far West, Garland found the Indian increasingly crucial to his design for critiquing the failure of American westerners to create a worthy civilization. But it took him a long time to discover precisely what Indian culture disclosed about the deficiencies of white civilization. Early in his Indian studies Garland himself thought he was dealing solely with the Indian problem—that is, how to help the Indian walk the white man's road and how to reform abuses of the reservation system. Only slowly did he realize that the Indian problem was primarily a white one.

Garland's fascination with the Indian began in a serious way with a trip to the Southwestern pueblos of Acoma, Isleta, Laguna, and Zuni in 1895. He then traveled back up to Montana and the Dakotas, then in 1900 down to Oklahoma, where he visited John Seeger to hear tales about the Indian way of life (Gish, p. 16). Later that year on the Standing Rock reservation he was fortunate enough to speak, through interpreters, with warriors of the late Sitting Bull. The novella "The Silent Eaters" comes out of this last experience. In all, Garland visited over a dozen reservations; gained the confidence of several Indian agents; and learned something about the conditions and feelings of American natives around the turn of the century. That education naturally focused his attention upon the pressing problems of assimilation and reservation abuses. Thus, it is no surprise that both *The Captain of the Gray-Horse Troop* and *The Book of the American Indian* are usually discussed in terms of those two issues. Indisputably, Garland was a reformer at heart; nor was he content to make his point in fiction. He also published a closely argued policy statement which proposed explicit alternatives to governmental policies administered on reservations.[3] And by the standards of American thinking in 1902, his proposals were penetrating and persuasive.

But as important as Garland's sleuthing of reservation ills was, it is not the sole issue in his Indian material. Rather he was on the track of a more substantive, if more subtle, question. Would civilization actually bring the defeated aborigines the good life? This problem, of course, has been with Western civilization ever since its technologically and numerically superior peoples have overrun others and imposed their standards upon them. Inevitably, the same disquieting question was working at the back of Garland's mind, and it gave a distinctively troubled cast to his Indian fiction. Its presence, indeed, creates the running dialogue that makes this work absorbing to today's reader.

Early, Garland's bottom-line belief was that the process of civilization was irreversible. He believed the imperative of social evolution dictated that the red man must henceforth walk the white man's road. But as a result of his observations on Indian reservations, Garland came to see that Indian ways had their own values; so he compromised by advocating that the Indian maintain his own identity while walking the road toward civilization. This more enlightened view, however, raised a number of paradoxes and forced Garland into a closer examination of Indian resistance. He became determined to discover "the soul of the Indian," as one of his fictive spokesmen put it. And at that point he opened himself to the seductive possibility that native life possessed a quality missing from, but perhaps necessary to, American civilization. Thus, Garland worked himself into that classic dilemma of double cultural vision which has been with our tradition ever since Sir Thomas More used Vespucci's account of the Inca empire to create a vision of an ideal society in *Utopia* (1517). And no less prestigious American predecessors than Cooper, Hawthorne, Thoreau, and Melville had at times suggested that native culture might be a viable referent against which basic failures of American culture could be judged.[4]

The best place to begin tracing Garland's search for the essential, and differentiating, essence of Indianness is an almost off-hand remark he wrote in a travel essay, "Hitting the Trail" (*McClure's Magazine*, 12 [February 1899], 298-304). In a brilliant synecdoche he compares the Indian trail with the white man's road. The red man's path is "always indirect, accommodating, patient of obstruction—an adjustment, not a ravage. It alarms nothing. It woos every wild thing. It never disfigures. It sacrifices itself. It loses itself in nature." Further, "the Trail is poetry; a wagon road is prose; the railroad, arithmetic." These images may be taken simply as romantic hyperbole directed invidiously against that supremely practical American temperament De Tocqueville despairingly noted.[5] They are that, but more. The synecdoche is so marvelously accurate about the quality of Indian thinking that even Levi-Strauss would be hard pressed to improve on it, although he devoted an entire volume to analyzing "the savage mind."[6]

As Garland traveled deeper into Indian country he learned more of its almost intangible quality. He recorded of his experiences there that "it has given me blessed release from care and worry and the troubled thinking of our modern day. It has been a return to the primitive and peaceful. Whenever the pressures of our complex city life thin my blood and benumb my brain, I seek relief on the trail; and when I hear the coyote waking to the yellow dawn my cares fall from me—I am happy" (*McClure's*, p. 304). It is this elusive peace of mind, happiness, which becomes the motif of his Indian fiction. And while he was no pioneer in discovering the paradox that civilization prized material advancement often at the expense of peace of mind, he recognized here a central objection of Indians to walking the white man's road.

Though Garland never quite resolved this paradox, a good share of his Indian fiction works in that direction. The key term, which eluded him, is what a more recent writer has called "quality." Robert Persig in *Zen and the Art of Motorcycle Maintenance*, has argued that quality is what our form of civilization conspicuously lacks. It emerges only when one is perfectly attuned to his environment and situation. As he says: "Peace of mind isn't at all superficial. . . . It's the whole thing. . . . The reason for this is that peace of mind is a prerequisite for a perception of that Quality which is beyond romantic Quality and classical Quality and which unites the two."[7] In Persig's view cultures tend to approach the world either in the romantic (intuitive) way or classical (analytical) way. He argues that Western tradition has been so obsessively rationalistic that is has failed to achieve a holistic sense of being, a caring identification with the environment. Untimately, this was the recognition towards which Garland was working. If technical advances could only be forced upon the Indian by inculcating him with the calculative mentality of white culture, he might be more victim than beneficiary. Thus, Garland tried to work out a concept which acknowledged the value of traditional Indian society and yet which showed how the Indian could benefit by civilization. As we follow his thinking through several key stories in *The Book of the American Indian* and selected episodes of *The Captain of the Gray-Horse Troop*, the overall direction of Garland's thought will become clear.

"Drifting Crane" was the first Indian story, appearing first in *Harper's* in 1890 before its collection in *The Book of the American Indian* (New York: Harper, 1923). Its dramatic effect is achieved by juxtaposing two representatives of the competing cultures in what amounts to a stereotypical white man versus red man confrontation. A white rancher moves out on newly taken Indian land and is visited by the local chief, Drifting Crane, who views him as an invader. Garland describes the meeting thus: "It was a thrilling, a significant scene. It was in absolute truth the meeting of the modern vidette of civilization with one of the rearguard of retreating barbarism. Each man was a type; each was wrong, and each was right. The Indian was as true and noble from the barbaric point of view as the white man. He was a warrior and a hunter; made so by circumstances over which he had no control" (p. 131). Here Garland has acknowledged the presence of two standards, barbaric and civilized; but clearly the latter is of a higher order. As Persig points out, the basic structure for all Western knowledge is a hierarchy. In this case, Garland simply follows Lewis Henry Morgan's hierarchy of social evolution: savage, barbaric, and civilized. The significant law here is that lower cultures have fewer human rights.

It takes Garland a while to locate the nature of cultural superiority. It is not found in the character of the rancher, although he is a courageous, not a vicious, person. Rather Garland says: "The settler represented the unflagging energy and fearless heart of the American pioneer. Narrow-minded, partly brutalized by hard labor and a lonely life, yet an admirable figure for all that. As he looked into the Indian's face he seemed to grow in height. He felt behind him all the weight of millions of westward-moving settlers; he stood the representative of an unborn state" (*Book*, p. 131). The fallacy of manifest destiny was not yet apparent to Garland, although the modern reader will see in this passage the rationale of one Western nation which used this philosophy to justify conquest, reservation-like concentration camps, and genocidal pogroms against an allegedly inferior race.

The settler then takes down his rifle from the wall. It is:

> The magazine rifle, most modern of guns; he patted the stock, pulled the crank, throwing a shell into view.
>
> "You know the thing, chief?" The Indian nodded slightly.
>
> "Well, I'll go when—this—is—empty." (*Book*, p. 131)

The images are perhaps the most revealing thing in the dialogue. White superiority is based upon force backed by technologial skill, especially in weaponry. Yet the rancher's machismo is disturbed by a curious note of ambivalence. Not oblivious of the great chief's dignity, he muses "there's land enough for us all, or ought to be. I don't understand—Well, I'll leave it to Uncle Sam." This would be the last time Garland let the ranchers off so easily. In later fiction they become a favorite bete noir, as they deliberately provoke reservation Indians into hostilities as an excuse for retaliatory preemption of more native land.

"The Story of Howling Wolf," first published in 1903, stands midway in philosophy between "Drifting Crane" and the concluding story, "The Silent Eaters." Here the traditionalist chief is transmuted into one ready to walk the white road, accepting the reservation agent, a just cavalry officer, as his role model. Carrying a note from the agent attesting to his peaceable character, Howling Wolf seeks to widen his experiences with white people by visiting a nearby town. Unfortunately, the townspeople have just been whipped by local yellow journalism into hysteria by false accounts of uprisings on the reservation. Howling Wolf is treacherously attacked and thrown in jail. And then tricked into thinking his freedom is being granted, he is ironically delivered into the hands of a mob during a Fourth of July celebration at which he is ridden down, beaten, dragged behind horses, mutilated, and left for dead. Miraculously, his iron constitution sustains him, but he is left a blind and bitter wreck of a once magnificent warrior. The savage irony of Howling Wolf's story suggests that Garland is beginning to think assimilation poses less of an Indian problem than a white one. The author's distrust of cowboys and ranchers, especially of the Far Western types observed in his travels, surfaces unmistakably. He is out to expose sensationally what he terms "the cruel, leering, racial hate of the border man, to whom the red man is big game" (*Book*, p. 149). Not only is the story an outraged protest against white brutality, it discloses that the Indian has become primarily a symbolic problem. Since he had, by this time, been defeated militarily and reduced to beggary on barren reservations, he posed no material threat. Garland intuits that something crucial lies beneath the continuing need to vindictively and falsely hound the very people one professes to be leading into a higher level of existence. He has no answer yet to this mystery.

The concluding tale in *The Book of the American Indian* is the novella "The Silent Eaters," which takes its name from Sitting Bull's trusted executive council, men of probity who eat in silence, disdaining any frivolity, while they meditate upon the difficulties of their chief's losing struggle to retain cultural hegemony for his defeated people. The narrator, Iapi, is son to one Silent Eater. He has been encouraged by Sitting Bull and Lieutenant Davies, a typical Garland military hero and intellectual, to learn about white ways. Davies, a man trained in classical logic, admonishes Iapi that "knowledge is power. . . . Study, acquire words, the white man's wisdom, then you will be able to defend the rights of your people" (p. 203). Sadly, by following this advice, Iapi becomes trapped between the opposing forces represented by Sitting Bull, the conservator of traditional values, and the Indian-hating agent, who is characterized by the author as "hard, unimaginative, and jealous of his authority. He was also a bigot and it is hard for anyone not a poet or a philosopher to be just to a people holding a different view of the world. Race hatred and religious prejudices stand like walls between the red man and the white" (*Book*, p. 253). Here Garland not only amplifies the note of cultural relativity sounded earlier, he suggests that civilization breeds racial and religious intolerance precisely because it has convinced all but poets and philosophers that its vision of civilized man is the only one. And to turn to Persig again, we see uncovered the commonest fallacy of classical thinking, the idea that of all alternative hypotheses about reality, there is only a single correct one (p. 160). Ergo, civilized man has the only true way of life and the only true religion. All other humans of all other persuasions are wrong, and their insistence upon false culture and religion simply verifies their unworthiness. They are a threat. When one understands this thinking, the antagonism toward all things Indian becomes a little clearer.

In "The Silent Eaters," then, an absolutist culture confronts and methodically sets out to destroy a pluralistic one. The reason is simply its inability to see the quality of pluralistic vision or the higher vision which Persig claims contains both with equanimity. And that is precisely the resolution Garland seeks—how the Indian can retain his vision and still assimilate white ways. But only in the character of the great Sitting Bull do we find the possibility of such transcendence, and he is adamantly opposed to assimilation, at least under the present circumstances. His character is most insightfully drawn. The Bull has been a shrewd and moral politician since his early manhood, an inveterate peacemaker who is brilliant in detecting and defusing threats against the wellbeing of the people, and a genius at ratiocination who empirically evalutes the evidence about the Ghost Dance and finds its validity wanting. Yet this paragon of wisdom, justice, and forebearance is destroyed by the viciousness of a conquering people determined to turn the vanquished into carbon copies of themselves. Sitting Bull, however, is allowed the last word on this issue, commenting tartly that if the Great Spirit had wanted Indians to be white people, he would have made them white. So much for the claim that there exists an hierarchal order of races.

Besides the character of Sitting Bull, we do not learn much about Indian personality and culture. One exception comes in the opening lines when Garland, this time poet rather than philosopher, invokes the tranquility of Plains life before the white man came. In the spring when grass sprang back to life, creeks flowed again, and the sun waxed warmer, there was a time of matchless beauty, harmony, and plenty. This seamless unity of beauty was matched by the serenity and peace of mind in Plains Indian villages. But later in the story, Garland hints that white people find these same golden plains hostile and lonely. There are indeed alternative realities. The white man carried on to the plains his antagonism to nature and subverted the natural order of things. This is the kind of progress Garland begins to find disturbing.

As a philosophic statement, "The Silent Eaters" exposes the mendacity of white protestations to improve the quality of barbaric life. The Sioux are systematically relocated to the poorest land, dispossessed of their horses and hunting gear, and dispersed from their communal village pattern once tribal leadership in governance and sacred ceremonies has been destroyed. Then they are asked to farm this worthless land, emulating the life patterns of the alienated and materialistic settlers who pushed them out. The final straw for many Indians was the implacable desire of agents, missionaries, and teachers to destroy in their children any respect for their elders or traditional values and beliefs. It is very difficult in this portrait, which was solidly grounded upon Garland's personal investigation of reservations. to find a key to assimilation without the loss of Indian integrity. Yet Garland was still convinced that if abuses were corrected, the best of the two worlds could be brought together. His before-mentioned article, "The Red Man's Present Needs," articulately sets before the American public the need and possibilities of such reform.

In the same year as this article, 1902, Garland also attempted to put his theories about bridging the two cultures into fictive action. His chief spokesman is Captain Curtis, the title hero in *The Captain of the Gray-*

Horse Troop (New York: Harper, 1902). The author's paternalism toward Indians is disappointingly obvious when Curtis's superior officer offers him an assignment as reservation agent: "You'll have a clear field for experiment at Smith. You can try all your pet theories on the Tetong." It would seem these Indians are reduced to little more than subjects of amateur experimentation in psycho-cultural engineering. This is not a promising start.

After Curtis takes over as agent, he and his ethnologist friend Lawson, as well as the young artist and aristocrat Elsie, debate the proper diagnosis and treatment of the Tetong problem. On one side are the enlightened men, on the other Elsie, who as daughter of the arch-conservative Senator Brisbane defends the genocidal assimilation approach of the U.S. War Department then administering the reservation system. Ultimately, Curtis wins the lovely Elsie to his side, though with a surprising concession, for she is artist enough to see that Curtis's rationalistic theories neglect the aesthetics of human life.

As Garland, through Curtis, struggles toward a principle to reconcile white and red realities, he first examines the doctrine of progress as Western peoples conceive it. Curtis muses that it may not be necessary for his Tetong charges to immediately, or ever, progress to the intensive agricultural and industrial techniques of Euro-Americans. Early in the novel he reflects that "the older I grow the less certain I am that any race or people has a monopoly of the virtues. I do not care to see the 'little people' of the world civilized in the way in which the word is commonly used. . . . If I could, I would civilize only to the extent of making life easier and happier—the religious beliefs, the songs, the native dress—all these things I would retain. What is life for, if not this?" (*Captain*, p. 81). While this judicious view moves Garland closer to the solution he seeks, an Indian might reply that Garland's assumptions are based upon a highly inaccurate history. It was the white man's arrival, introduction of European diseases, and wholesale seizure of land that destroyed for Indians their easy and happy life. But Garland was working toward an important principle. If the Indians themselves could determine which elements of foreign culture they wanted to adopt, a healthy balance between red and white might be struck. After all, the Sioux had radically transformed their society by integrating the European horse. Incidentally, one should note that Captain Curtis actually subverts his espousal of retaining native customs. Only at special ceremonies are the Tetong encouraged to wear native garb and remember their traditions.

In fact, Garland had not done his homework well at all. He pictures the frustrating difficulties of getting the Tetongs to become farmers. While it is probably true they relied extensively during the past hundred years upon a hunting economy, they were by no means ignorant of agriculture. But the exasperated agent Curtis maligns the intellectual capacity and motivation of red people. Though the Tetong have faithfully planted unfamiliar crops according to Curtis's instructions, they just cannot get the hang of farming: "These child-like souls said: 'Behold we have done our part, now let Mother Earth and Father Sun bring forth the harvest. We cannot ripen the grain; we can only wait. Besides we are weary' " (*Captain*, p. 398). In short, they are too lazy to weed and cultivate their crops by the workaholic standards of white people. Nor do they grasp the nature of a plant's life cycle: "The seed and the apple are too far apart" in time for them to see the connection. As we know now, and Garland should have been able to discover from narratives of exploration, Indian botanists were among the foremost in the world. They had domesticated numerous plants like maize before the dawn of European civilization. In fact, over four-sevenths of the United States' present agricultural produce is from Indian-developed crops.

By pandering to the worst suspicions of his audience about Indian intellective capacity, Garland measurably weakens the case for equitable treatment. If Indians are genetically and culturally thousands of years behind white people, how can the differences be bridged by simply eliminating abuses on reservations? And how can the Indian expect to be assimilated on equal terms? Garland's answer is to go slow. As Captain Curtis explains: "They have developed like ourselves through countless generations of life under relatively stable conditions. These moderial conditions are giving way, are vanishing, but the mental traits they formed will persist. Think of this when you are impatient with them" (*Captain*, p. 138). This passage represents a vacillation back to Garland's earlier belief that white civilization is destined to make over the rest of the world in its image. He failed to indicate here, as he well knew, that the scientific approach of Western culture has severe limitations in providing the good life. As Persig has noted, Western-style rationality has worked very well since the Renaissance. And "so long as the need for food, clothing, and shelter is dominant [the scientific approach] will continue to work" (p. 110). But he warns that when such needs no longer overwhelm people, they will discover that "the whole structure of reason, handed down to us from ancient times, is no longer adequate. It begins to be seen for what it really is—emotionally hollow, esthetically meaningless and spiritually empty" (p. 110).

Garland is manifestly dissatisfied with Curtis's advice, since it ignores Western civilization's deficiencies, the prime target of his earlier fiction. But he is in a quandry about how the Tetong should be led along the white man's road. The best he can do is have Captain Curtis vow to stay on the reservation "till I can demonstrate my theory that, properly led, the people can be made happy" (*Captain*, p. 153). And a few pages later we learn what that entails: "To be clean, to be peaceful, to be happy—these are precepts I would teach them" (p. 159). Unfortunately for Garland, he has the whole thing backwards. The Tetongs were undoubtedly cleaner, more peaceful, and happier folks before civilization arrived. However, it is true that once they have been deprived of their considerable land base, they needed to learn something about the scientific approach in order to survive.

Garland does intuit the unnerving possibility of Indians becoming totally rational like whites. They will undoubtedly then lose their aesthetic and spiritual sensibilities as Persig suggests Western civilization did after the Renaissance. Garland's recognition of this vital truth appears when Captain Curtis chides Elsie for painting an old Tetong as a mindless Indian beggar. Curtis insists that "Crawling Elk is the annalist and story teller of his tribe. He carries the 'winter count' and the sacred page, and can tell you of every movement of the Tetongs for more than a century and a half. His mind is full of poetry, and his conceptions of the earth and sky are beautiful. He knows little that white men know, and cares for very little that the white man fights for, but his mind teems with the lore of the mysterious universe into which he has been thrust, and which he has studied for seventy-two years. In the eyes of God, I am persuaded there is no great difference between old Crawling Elk and Herbert Spencer. The circle of Spencer's knowledge is wider, but is as far from including the infinite as the redman's story of creation" (*Captain*, pp. 100-101). And a moment later, Curtis concludes: "All these things, and many more, you must learn before you can represent the soul of the redman. You can't afford to be unjust" (p. 101). Nor does Garland wish to be unfair. This long paragraph was as close as he would come to granting the Indian a complete, independent, and poetic construction of reality second only to that produced by the best mind of the Western world. That was more than almost any other white writer or anthropologist of the time would allow. Its weakness, as Persig would tell us, is that one cannot create a hierarchy of poetic and rational constructions of reality (p. 243). They are inherently equal and complementary. Somehow they need to be combined: the red man's direct apprehension of nature's unity and the white man's breaking down nature into controllable entities.

In an effort to amalgamate both the poetic and rational modes, Garland reaches for a principle capable of that synthesis. Sensing that the essential quality of Indian life lies in the realm of aesthetics, but beyond language, Garland has Captain Curtis finally acknowledge the deficiency of a purely intellectual solution to the Indian (or for that matter, white) problem. Curtis confesses to his artistic fiancee, "you've given me a dim notion of a new philosophy. I haven't organized it yet, but it's something like this: Beauty is a sense of fitness, harmony. This sense of beauty—call it taste—

demands positively a readjustment of the external facts of life, so that all angles, all suffering and violence, shall cease. If all men were lovers of the beautiful, the gentle, then the world would needs be suave and genial, and life harmoniously colored, like your own studio, and we would campaign only against ugliness. *To civilize would mean a totally different thing.* I'm not quite clear on my theory yet, but perhaps you can help me out" [my italics] (*Captain*, p. 330). Philosophically speaking, this is the high point of *The Captain of the Gray-Horse Troop*. But Elsie proves quite unable to help Curtis develop his insight, which is frittered away in the remaining pages of the novel.

In a remarkably parallel passage from *Zen and the Art of Motorcycle Maintenance*, Persig supplies the explanation Garland sought. Persig too finds ugliness pervasive, the real enemy of the good life. But he argues that ugliness does not reside in modern technology nor its materials: "Real ugliness lies in relationships between people who produce the technology and the things they produce, which results in a similar relationship between the people who use the technology and the things they use" (p. 284). By this he means that in the West products of technology are not created out of a sense of identity between the craftsman and the material: "It is this identity [which non-Western people have] that modern, dualistically conceived technology lacks" (p. 284). In short, ugliness of spirit is what plagues Western civilization. By a curious paradox, once nature has been reduced to the manipulatable, material level, it becomes ordinary. And while it can be made to yield the physical aspects of the good life, its sacredness is lost. As Curtis noticed, the Tetong winced at the idea of tearing the breast of mother earth with a plow. It violated their carefully developed sense of identity with nature.

Persig believes the impasse between these disparate approaches can be hurdled. He argues that "the way to solve the conflict between human values and technological needs is not to run away from technology. That's impossible. The way to resolve the barriers of dualistic thought that prevent a real understanding of what technology is—not exploitation of nature, but a fusion of nature and the human spirit into a new kind of creation that transcends both" (p. 284). He adds that every dimension of human existence involves problems which admit of either a beautiful or ugly solution. To achieve beauty, Persig explains just what civilizing means, the principle for which Curtis groped. The requirements are "both an ability to see what 'looks good' [the Indian's well-developed aesthetic sensibility] and an ability to understand the underlying methods to arrive at that 'good' [the white man's scientific method]" (p. 285).

Therefore, we can conclude that Garland came very close to an understanding of the real issues involved in assimilation of Indian people. He would have come full circle to recognize that the Indian world needed less from the white world than vice versa, although both could have profited from each other. But the old Indian life, whose beauty Garland so keenly appreciated, was already whole and complete, being based upon a spiritual sense of identity with the material/spiritual world. Ugliness of spirit was discouraged there, nature was revered rather than exploited, and one's fellow man was respected despite his race or creed. The aboriginal Sioux and Tetong may have been inferior in material possessions, but not in things of the spirit.

Pushed to its logical conclusion, *The Captain of the Gray-Horse Troop* is a continuation of Garland's earlier criticism of our failure to establish a worthy civilization in America. Had we learned from the first Americans how to limit technology so it did not diminish man's identity with the wondrous world around him, there would not be the ugliness of spirit that so enraged Garland—the avariciousness of land-hungry ranchers, the leering racial brutality of drunken cowboys, the crookedness of traders, and the sanctimoniousness of missionaries and other emissaries of white culture who despised the very people they attempted to help. To Garland's credit, he opened a fruitful trail for later critics of our national culture. And his intuition that the Indian was crucial to understanding our failed culture proved perfectly accurate.[8]

Notes

1. See Robert Gish, *Hamlin Garland: The Far West* (Boise, Idaho: Boise State Univ., 1976), Jay Martin, *Harvests of Change: American Literature, 1865-1914* (Englewood Cliffs: Prentice-Hall, 1967), and Donald Pizer, "Hamlin Garland (1860-1940)," *American Literary Realism*, 1 (Fall 1967), 45-51.

2. Hamlin Garland, "The West in Literature," *Arena*, 6 (November 1892), 669-76.

3. "The Redman's Present Needs," *The North American Review*, 174 (April 1902), 476-88. This essay was reprinted by *NAR*, 258 (Winter, 1973), 90-95.

4. Edwin Fussell makes this point especially well in *Frontier: American Literature and the American West* (Princeton, N.J.: Princeton Univ. Press, 1965).

5. Alexis de Tocqueville, *Democracy in America*. See Phillips Bradley's two-volume edition published in 1942.

6. Claude Levi-Strauss, *The Savage Mind* (Chicago: Univ. of Chicago Press, 1966).

7. Robert M. Persig, *Zen and the Art of Motorcycle Maintenance* (New York: Bantam Books, 1974).

8. For two rather different discussions of Garland's Indian materials the reader might want to examine Roy W. Meyer, "Hamlin Garland and the American Indian," *Western American Literature*, 2 (Summer 1967), 109-25, and Owen J. Reamer, "Garland and the Indians," *New Mexico Quarterly*, 34 (Autumn 1964), 257-80.

A Herder's Life in South Dakota: The Cipher Diary of Archer B. Gilfillan

AUSTIN J. MCLEAN

Austin J. McLean, chief of special collections and rare books at the University of Minnesota Libraries, has also published on Gilfillan in the South Dakota Review.

On the night of December 2, 1924, Archer B. Gilfillan started a diary written in cipher: "I am going to begin a diary in which I shall put down exactly what I think and do, without fear of its being read and consequently with all the honesty of which I am capable. . . . Had an easy day today, but the sheep are restless on the bedground. A coyote got a lamb the night before last and I think he is back again. I expected him." Archer was writing by lantern light in a sheep wagon on the AD Ranch, which covered about nineteen square miles just west of the Slim Buttes in the northwestern corner of South Dakota, where he had been employed as a herder for eight years by Al Dean.

For his occupation Archer had an unusual background. His father was an Episcopalian clergyman, and Archer was raised in a genteel and unworldly environment. In 1910 he graduated from the University of Pennsylvania and was awarded Phi Beta Kappa. Later, after failing as a homesteader in South Dakota, he attended the Episcopal Seminary in Chicago for three years. He then began his career as a sheep herder which lasted seventeen years.

He maintained the diary for eight years and four months, a period that spanned his life from his thirty-eighth year until he was forty-seven. He wrote on standard letter-size paper. A day's entry might cover from one to ten or more pages. The diary consists of 9,010 manuscript pages divided into twenty-five volumes. Although he claims at times in the diary that he has never yet failed to make a record for each day, a few gaps exist. Presumably the pages were lost before he had them bound; a diarist in a sheep wagon sometimes had problems. Several times he mentions that a strong wind came up and blew loose pages from the wagon, and he had to chase after them across the prairie. Some years after Archer's death in 1955, his sister, Emily Heilman, gave the diary and other material to the University of Minnesota Library. John Jenson, Rare Books Librarian, transcribed it, completing the task in 1977.

Each year on the date when he began the diary, Gilfillan usually included in that day's entry comments about his diary or other diarists. On December 2, 1927 he wrote, "This is the third birthday of my diary. . . . We live in a real world but we pretend to live in quite a different one. My diary deals with the real world, and hence has to be written in cipher. . . . As regards obscenity, I have neither sought it nor avoided it. . . . If the emphasis herein seems to be on the obscene it is merely because we supress that side altogether in ordinary writing." In his attempt to set down honestly what he does and thinks he is merciless towards himself, but generally merciful towards others because he cannot know their minds.

The diary covers his main achievement in life, which was writing *Sheep*, published in 1929. Its graphic prose still makes that book fascinating reading today. In *Sheep*, following a picturesque description of the land where he herds, he wrote: "Strange it would be if the all-pervading calm did not bring with it an interior peace" (p. 20). The diary, on the other hand, is filled with expressions of worry, distress, and torment, but there is scarcely any reference to "interior peace." Perhaps the closest approximation to it for the diarist occurred when he wrote, "A feeling of utter content suffused me as I have not felt for a long time." But he experienced this while standing on the back platform of a train just after starting on vacation. He also once described a sense of luxurious peace while staying at the ranch, but it was in a dream: "This morning I was dreaming that I was sitting in a stuffed armchair in an exclusive club just lighting a cigar when I heard the boss rattling the stove downstairs."

The bulk of the diary deals with his life as a herder, day after day through the changing seasons. The reader gets a sense of Archer's solitary place in the vast land where he herds. He learns that Archer walks several miles toward some stray sheep which he discovers are antelope, or that he sees a car approaching which proves to be only a shadow on a distant hill. Frequently a day's account begins, "I saw no one today." This sentence often is qualifed to read, "I saw no one today to talk to." He may mention having seen a rider on a ridge or a car or wagon on the grade.

He always described the movement of the sheep each day and their general behavior. For easy days he might write, "Today the sheep practically herded themselves." For difficult days he might write: "The sheep ran like deer." "The sheep ran the whole morning as if they were possessed." "The first thing the sheep did this morning was split and go in exactly different directions." "It was an endless battle with the sheep today." "The big bunch simply exploded all over the landscape."

In presenting his life as a herder, Gilfillan often achieves greater immediacy in the diary than in the book. An early winter morning: "Last night was the coldest yet this winter. I was warm in bed (I let the dog sleep on the bed all night) but when I got up this morning I could hardly stand it. My feet ached on account of the cold floor. I poured kerosene on the wood but it was three-quarters of an hour before the wagon was warm enough to eat breakfast. My fried potatoes, set just behind the stove, were frozen stiff, the oatmeal was frozen, and the coffee had a scum of ice on it. I was late getting the sheep out."

A hot summer afternoon:

> I got dinner and then passed one of the most wretched afternoons in a long while. There was an intense muggy heat, with little wind, but it blew directly from a badly decayed sheep, filling the wagon with stench. My water was low, all I had being the dregs of the barrel, yellow and unappetizing, but I had to drink constantly. The flies poured in the wagon by the hundreds. My two fly killers not being anywhere nearly able to take care of them, I attacked them from time to time with my broken fly-swatter. Finally at six o'clock, sick to my stomach with the never-ending stench, I rode to the east end of the sheep and stayed there till sunset.

Usually he visits with a few people in the course of a day. His boss, Al Dean, regularly brings him provisions and instructions. He chats with nearby herders, neighbors stop by on various errands, and people always seem to be roaming around looking for stray horses or cattle and they spend time with him. He is regularly invited to supper at the ranch or at neighboring ranches or at homes in Buffalo. A favorite expression of his is "It was a feast and I ate to repletion." He frequently provides dinner or supper to herders and other visitors. Sometimes the meal he gets in return is not a feast, as in the following case, where a lunch is brought out to him on a point from which he can observe the sheep:

> I kept getting hungrier all the time but it was an hour and a half before Fred finally returned. Instead of the crackers and cheese which I had asked him to bring he brought eight eggs fried in a skillet, a bottle of preserves and a loaf of bread, also three potatoes lying in a pork sauce made from strong boar meat already four years old. I took a dead fly from the pork sauce. I saw him take one from the preserves. The eggs tasted of a thousand former repasts prepared in that unwashed skillet, and if I hadn't been ravenously hungry I could never have eaten anything. As it was I suppressed nausea by an effort of will and ate a full meal.

He usually reads at specific times during the course of the day and sometimes late at night. He also comments about the books he reads. Of Mary Austin's *The Flock*, he wrote, "I finished *The Flock*. I see no reason to change my first opinion of it. There is page after page of pure bull shit. She never uses one word if she can use ten to express the same idea. She never uses a word in its right meaning if she can distort another to take its place."

He corresponded with many people and eagerly awaited the delivery of mail. Sometimes he would transcribe into the diary expecially interesting or important letters he had received or sent, or verses or jokes from them. On March 16, 1929, the day he received word that his book was accepted for publication, he wrote a long letter to Anita Loos (author of *Gentlemen Prefer Blondes*, 1925), which began, "My first (and I fear my last) book has just been accepted for publication by the Atlantic Monthly Press. I wrote every word of this book with your picture in front of me for inspiration, and for this inspiration I wish to thank you." There is no reference to a reply in the diary.

Card playing was a principal recreation, as the following excerpt suggests:

> I got an early supper and had just finished when Johnny came along. He had a coyote skin tied on behind his saddle. He had run him a mile and a half till he lay down and then kicked him to death. In spite of my good resolutions we began to play poker, draw and then stud, and when we stopped I was just five dollars loser. This made me owe Johnny fifteen dollars and twenty-three cents in all. I told him that I was through for good and would pay him when I could. I have lost five dollars and wasted an evening.

Archer undoubtedly was the worst poker player in Harding County. Everyone beat him, but he could resist playing only for brief periods of time. One suspects, and at times Archer suspected, that some men came to the wagon to take money from him rather than to enjoy his companionship. While playing poker he usually compounded his natural disadvantage by getting drunk. His herding wages were sixty dollars a month, and he was always well over a thousand dollars in debt. He began writing articles for magazines in order to try to pay off debts.

Innumerable entries contain references to his drinking and drunkenness. One of his standard lines is: "I went down to where the jug was cached and took my regular seven-swallow drink." He tests the liquor obtained from a bootlegger: "I took a five-swallow drink . . . and the bite of its fiery flavor convinced me that it had not been diluted." He drinks too much: "I staggered around awhile in front of the wagon, circling cactus beds and wandering aimlessly and then went in and went to bed without lighting the lantern or eating a bite of supper and leaving the two-gallon jug of hooch beside the wagon wheel." He is ill the next morning: "The first thing I did this morning was to throw up. I certainly felt wretched." In keeping with the stated purpose of his diary he does not shrink from presenting himself in any disgraceful situation, as in this incident on a trip to the Black Hills: "I took a hell of a big drink and the rest of the canyon trip is more or less confused. I remember passing innumerable cars and that Charlie once had to patch a tire and I got out and tripped and fell flat in the weeds and lay there till Charlie finished with the tire and helped me up."

As he recounts his life, Archer also tells about the social life and customs of the time in Harding County and hears much gossip which he sets down in his diary: "Mrs. Dean told me that Tom Barns' bride of three months came down to a dance in Ludlow with another married man and got drunk and fell over the ash pile. Tom went to Bowman today to see about it." Sometimes the reader learns of shocking events, briefly sketched: "I saw a rider coming from the direction of the wagon. It was Ole. He was all excited about two Holy Rollers, preachers, that had been holding services at Swain's and Robins'. He said that last night they went out to tar and feather one of the preachers but he got away and went to Swain's. They followed him there and Swain drove them off with a shotgun."

At times Archer serves as a confidant for troubled people:

> This morning I pushed the sheep east, having tired of the endless chase when they start west. They moved very leisurely and I was still in the wagon when Bill Hall rode up. I saw at once there was something strange about him. . . . He told me that Sid Johnson stayed overnight at his place a few days ago while he was away, and that Sid came downstairs at four in the morning and tried to screw Kate. She told him to go on about his business and promised that if he would leave her alone she would not tell Bill. She made Bill promise, before she told him, that he would not do anything about it. Bill said he had been wondering since whether Sid was trying to get even with him for the number of times that he had screwed Alice since she married Sid. He said that Alice had tried to get money out of him several times, claiming that one of the girls was his.

In reading *Sheep* one probably gets the impression that the author is a rough, keenly observant, high-spirited outdoorsman. The diary presents a different personality. He is impractical, insecure, kind, weak, and extraordinarily sensitive.

Archer was short and fat, and he got fatter as he grew older. Even though he walked long distances with the sheep he could not work off his huge starchy meals ("I ate macaroni, raisins, doughnuts and candy, a good dinner."). Once while staying at the ranch he wrote, "During the morning I went into the Deans' bedroom for something and happening to see myself in the full-length glass I received a big shock. I am fatter than I ever have been in my life or ever expected to be. I could not believe my eyes."

When meeting people, especially women, he was keenly aware of the impression he made. On meeting a young woman, he wrote, "I was introduced to her, obviously not to her intense delight." About an incident in a hotel in Rapid City he wrote, "The hotel clerk, a mild inoffensive man, told me how he had killed ten Greeks in a race riot in Chicago. It is no compliment to be lied to that way." In response to a tall tale by a stranger who stopped at the sheep wagon, Archer wrote, "I wish so many people wouldn't pick me to lie to. It doesn't speak well for my appearance."

Archer was alert to the proprieties, whether he was in the sheep wagon with visitors or as a guest at someone's home. While driving two hundred yearling sheep, which Al Dean had purchased, from Ludlow to the ranch, he stayed overnight at a ranch on the way as was the custom:

> He took me upstairs and showed me a bed with clean sheets. When I came to undress I was horrified to see that my legs were simply black with dirt. I had sweat all day and walked most of the time and as I was wearing nothing in summer but shirt and overalls the dust had settled and stuck and I was afraid of dirtying the bed. But everyone had retired and I could not very well go downstairs and rummage around for towels, water and soap. So I had to take the chance and had some troubled dreams of visiting a wealthy family and privately sending my sheets and blankets to the laundry, only to be discovered by my hostess.

Archer would not tolerate certain vulgar practices:

> I was just putting a cold supper on the table when August came in the old Ford. He asked me if I had heard about Carl Swenson and told me that he was at present in jail at Buffalo for knocking up his seventeen year old daughter. This is the third case we have had of that sort in this county in the last five years. . . . I knew Swenson when I worked at Gilbert's during lambing one year. I took a dislike to him because while he and I lay in a double bed talking he let a fart like an exploding mine. I detest that filthy habit and dislike anyone who indulges in it in the presence of another.

On holidays Archer sometimes attended dances. Of an incident at a dance on the Fourth of July, which further reveals his sense of decorum, he wrote, "I was watching the dancers when Claude stooped behind me, and reaching around me he goosed the woman directly in front of me. When she turned around I did the worst possible thing. I said, 'Excuse me.' I left there immediately and went to the other end of the hall."

For many years Archer herded daily some fifteen hundred sheep. He knew all the ways of death for sheep, from coyote bites to drowning, but he never became inured to suffering in sheep or other animals. On the death of one sheep he wrote, typically, "An old ewe died, one that the shearers had cut badly. Her shoulders were a mass of maggots in spite of the fact that we had treated all the cuts with pine tar. It was a horrible death to die."

Sometimes a sheep dog had to be killed, but in this instance not by Archer:

> We went back to the rocky hill and there he told me he had orders to shoot Sport. I knew Sport had to go, because as a sheep dog he is an outlaw and it would be impossible to train Trixie as long as he was present. But I was sorry to see Sport go because he has worked with me and stayed with me. So when Tony tied him preparatory to shooting him I walked down in the badlands. But I heard the shot that killed him and the tears rolled down my cheeks. When Tony rejoined me I was still crying. He had a pop bottle full of hooch and I took a big drink and after awhile that steadied me. We hunted for rabbits but could not find any.

At times he witnesses flagrant cruelty to animals, as in this case of an old homesteader who sometimes is mentally unsound:

> I reached Moberg's shortly before noon. When I went into his dugout to get warm I saw a dead dog lying on a box. I asked him what was the matter and he told me that he had lost all three dogs in the last two days. I found that he had suspected Frans Lyons of poisoning them, but since all three died curled up naturally it could hardly be that. What killed them was plain starvation and exposure. They were like living skeletons when I saw them two days ago, and when Moberg told me that the last dog to die ate greedily on one of the others I was convinced that this was the case. Of course Moberg is not responsible as other men are but it is terrible to think of animals suffering like that. . . . I stayed at Moberg's only a few minutes, being horrified and disgusted about the dogs.

In his forty-sixth year Archer wrote, "It is too bad that of the three or four women who have been more than passingly interested in me, not one of them was of interest to me." He craved love and affection from women, but their likely rejection of him deranged his relations with them. However, he found great pleasure in the presence of beautiful young women, and often sketches them rapturously:

> When I saw Irene I was struck dumb. When I last saw her she was simply a passable girl but now I saw a startling beauty. Her yellow hair hung almost to her shoulders, her complexion was the clearest pink and white, her teeth were perfect and her eyes large and of the clearest blue. She had wonderful breasts, jutting and trembling. Sit-

> ting in the kitchen, instead of out at work where he belonged, was Ed's hired man who was to run the place, with Irene, for the three weeks Ed expected to be gone. . . . How any mother could leave her sixteen-year-old daughter, a raving beauty at that, alone on a farm with an eighteen year old farm hand of trashy antecedents, is something I will never be able to fathom. I would not give a plugged nickel for the virtue of any girl so situated after one week, let alone three.

His observations about women are usually limited to their breasts, and the diary is filled with brief descriptions of their sizes and shapes. One extraordinary comment may suffice: "She had breasts that make your mouth water and your hands twitch."

The sale of his book *Sheep* did not give Archer financial independence, as he sometimes dreamed that it might. He quickly spent the money he received and remained in debt. After the publication of his book he gave a number of lectures and acquired a reputation as a witty speaker. Having become well known in Harding County he decided to run for county treasurer, with the hope of earning a good salary and living in town. He ran against the incumbent and was beaten badly. He reported his feelings that night of the election, May 3, 1932, in his diary after he had returned from town to the bunkhouse at the ranch:

> I could not go to sleep. I was conscious of a physical ache in my chest. My whole life seemed to be in ruins. I had been almost sure for the past two years of winning office and living in Buffalo. The defeat was apparently so crushing that it not only killed my political hopes for the present but for any time in the future. . . . It was after two o'clock before I dropped into the slumber of mental and spiritual exhaustion. I slept only about an hour and then woke again to the pain of the realization and lay awake till it was time to get up. The Juhalas asked me how the election came out and Waino made the rather unsympathetic remark, "I guess you will keep on herding sheep."

His friends had warned him, before and after the election, that his drinking hurt his chances for winning, but he continued to drink more heavily than ever before. On August 11, 1932, he wrote, "I hate to record this day's doings worse than any that have gone into this diary in seven years." In a long and pathetic account he tells how he was discovered drunk in the wagon that morning. He was not fired, but later he was relieved from herding and was allowed to do chores at the ranch for his board. On December 2, 1932, the eighth anniversary of his diary, he wrote, "On this anniversary I am lower in worldly position than I have been yet. The book sale has practically ended, I am dead politically, I have lost my sixteen year long job, and I am discredited in my chosen occupation. I am working all day every day for my board."

Relations between Al Dean and Archer always worsened when he lived in the ranch house or bunkhouse any length of time. This continued when he was working there for his board. Once they had a violent argument while Archer was shoveling manure in the barn, and Al almost hit Archer. Regarding this incident, Archer concluded, "My poor showing in the encounter occasioned me no shame, because I have always known that there is no fight in me."

He secured another herding job nearby in the spring of 1933. The diary ends in mid-sentence, on April 6, before he left the AD Ranch. One quotation from the diary may well sum up Archer's view of the world. In a newspaper office of a small town he once met an ordinary woman who was about his own age, and he later wrote, "We sized each other up, I think with mutual disappointment."

"Intimate Immensity": Mythic Space in the Works of Laura Ingalls Wilder

DOLORES ROSENBLUM

Dolores Rosenblum, an assistant professor at the State University of New York, Albany, is on leave this year as an Andrew Mellon Post-Doctoral Fellow, writing a critical study of Christina Rossetti.

In the series of chronicles of a frontier childhood that have come to be known as the "Little House" books, Laura Ingalls Wilder does what all innovative novelists do: she defamiliarizes the known and familiarizes the unknown. Her writing generates the kind of paradox indicated in the title of this paper, that "intimate immensity" defined by Gaston Bachelard, the French critic and master day-dreamer who never saw an American plain, but who would have understood immediately its power as an image.[1] Writing from the point of view of a child, Wilder builds the world from the ground up, representing both the domestic and the wild as excitingly strange and comfortingly intimate. Thus she breathes new life into our conceptions of such familiar phenomena as "bed," "table," "chair," "house" and "town." Conversely, she makes imaginatively habitable a territory that seems literally to have been uninhabited until her protagonist sets foot in it, inconceivable until she thinks it.

Laura Ingalls Wilder makes sense of child Laura Ingalls' prairie world by organizing empty space around actual structures—a variety of "little houses," ranging from the covered wagon to the "real house with two stories, and glass windows."[2] Given the security and essential changelessness of these little houses, Laura can venture out into the open and return and venture out again, engaging in the real tasks of childhood. To grow up in that particular culture she must wash dishes and sweep and sit silent and decorous on Sundays; she must also observe—gophers, prairie chickens, the perfect circle of the sky curving down to the level land; and she must dream—of being a wild pony or a naked Indian child.

"Let me tell you the way it really was," is Wilder's implicit pact with the reader, and so usually we are first impressed by the delightful "machinery" of the books. Like intricate toys whose working parts are entirely visible, these accounts please us by the satisfying fit of one part into another, especially in the sober yet playful representations of the workaday world. For a child, play is authentic work, and "real" work can be the best kind of play. Hence as if from a magically jargon-free manual we learn about the complicated processes by which men and women cultivate nature: the metamorphic steps of cheese-making, the crude and subtle labors of building a log cabin, the orchestration of men and wagons and horses to make a railroad cut. We also discover how a nineteenth-century little girl must wear restrictive layers of clothing even while camping out on the prairie; how a resourceful woman can make "apple" pie out of green pumpkin and "chicken" pie out of the blackbirds that have devastated the corn and oat crops; how a lucky and provident man can survive, buried in a snow-cave, a three-day blizzard, or avert a prairie fire that is advancing "faster than a horse can run" (*Little House on the Prairie,* New York: Harper and Row, 1953, p. 277).

Beyond the accumulation of pragmatic detail, however, we "see" with Laura's eyes the "big white shining clouds" float "high up in clear space" (*Little House on the Prairie*, p. 274); the seemingly level prairie collapse into unexpected hollows, buffalo wallows overgrown with violets; the stars hang low from the bowl of the sky. That is, the narrator gives us precise instructions about the aesthetic, emotional and moral as well as practical dimensions of her world. Yet Wilder's aesthetic "constructions," her well-made and repetitive formulations, have a mythic resonance, rooted as they are in certain binary oppostions that are basic to our ways of experiencing the world and organizing our perceptions. Laura's world can be categorized fairly easily by a series of interdependent oppositions, though the order of the following sequence is by no means inevitable:

inner	outer	rational	irrational
(house)	(prairie)	restraint	freedom
known	unknown	work	play
human	non-human	regularity	irregularity
order	chaos	contentment	excitement
culture	nature	staying in one place	moving on
civilized	wild	possession	relinquishment

Further, Wilder generates at least two sets of oppositions which cut across the basic inner/outer schema, and which are less inert than the above categories. The members of the pairs fullness and emptiness, sound and silence, stand in a particularly dynamic relation to one another. Emptiness is the potential for fullness, silence the potential for sound—one state always tends towards the other. Thus one "cosmic" plot of these narratives is "to fill the emptiness," whether by cultivating the land and inhabiting it, or by discovering the diversity of its teeming life. Another is "to fill the silence," whether by speaking and making music, or by discovering the variety of natural sounds—wolf cry, panther scream, blizzard screech, the rustle of grasses in the gentle wind.

The basic "human" plot of all the narratives, however, is "to survive," that is, to learn the rules—and internalize them as self-regulation—so that you can enjoy life as a civilized human. Learning the rules means learning how to "read" the world, or rather how to make the world signify, usually through the kind of mental operations which yield both the abstractions and the metaphors suggested in the preceding list. Wilder's central metaphor for the process of human survival and development always involves the problem of inhabiting space: how do you fill with your presence an emptiness that threatens to efface you? The narratives thus are organized around a variety of habitations constructed against and in compliance with the vast outer space surrounding the human figures. That space is both threatening and inviting—the true American sublime.

Ultimately Wilder converts both configurations—inner and outer space, house and prairie—into what Bachelard has called "felicitous space" (p. xxxi). There the creative imagination can range freely while remaining securely anchored. More precisely, the child Laura can move relatively freely between house and the open, the domestic order and "coziness" of the former functioning as an internalized system that allows her both to regulate herself (though with some near-miss adventures) and to feel the immensity of the latter as something like intimate. The radical oppositions composing Laura's world are never reconciled, however. Rather, by the play of the imagination the writer/protagonist performs the necessary act of mediation. Though not simultaneously, the child Laura can experience and the writer Wilder can project the emptiness and loneliness of the prairie on the one hand; on the other, the spiritual expansion which the literal expanse mirrors and inspires. Similarly, the house can metamorphose on occasion from life-sustaining central hearth to a prison for the senses.

At especially felicitous moments, however, the mediation does break down boundaries, transposing one territory upon the other. Through Laura's perceptions Wilder creates a middle ground where outer and inner converge, even intermingle; and a time which is both an eternal *now* and a nostalgically remembered *then*. The clearest models of this middle space occur in the volume *Little House on the Prairie.* This account gives us a prairie which is both vast and intimate, empty and dense with life, chaotic and yet suggestive of another kind of order. It also presents us with the moving house—the covered wagon. Just as one kind of play-house depends on the imaginative transformation of one order of objects into another—foliage into a roof, stumps or pumpkins into chairs—the covered wagon demonstrates a kind of practical play. Hickory bows and a canvas cover convert it into a "house" that can easily turn into a simple wagon again. Perhaps the covered wagon as house is so satisfying because it fulfills our archaic desire to have it both ways, to move yet stay in one place, to change yet stay the same.

The covered wagon frames the book; the central third details the building of the little house on the Kansas prairie, an arduous yet satisfying process of fitting one part into another. This adult, "real-life" counterpart of children's play still involves metamorphic transformations: lengths of logs into walls, chunks of big logs into chairs, stones and mud into a chimney, earth swept clean into a floor, "holes" into windows and a door. Building a house thus requires not simply the manipulation of physical objects according to an architectural blueprint, but as well a shift in vision according to mental diagrams of another order. The stumps are in fact no longer stumps but chairs, and the china shepherdess Ma carefully positions on the rough mantel is not merely a civilized nicety, but an agent of culture.

The mental diagrams that all the Ingalls bring to bear on the making of their little house on the prairie, derive in part from a prior "actual" model—the cabin of *Little House in the Big Woods* (New York:Harper and Row, 1953). The Ingalls have left their well-stocked little house in the woods of Wisconsin because Pa has begun to feel spiritually crowded, and because where there are too many people wild animals won't stay and the family won't have enough to eat. The little house in the woods, with its attic where Laura and Mary play house amidst pumpkins, onions, herbs, hams and venison, is as much a store-house as a shelter, and much of this volume deals with the procuring of food and the process of rendering the "raw" edible. It is also "neat and pretty," the scene of Ma's order-making. In all the volumes the disposition of furnishings according to the exigencies of space and the claims of taste is meticulously described. Curtains (usually transformed from old sheets and dresses), tablecloth, the china shepherdess and the intricate bracket Pa carves lovingly for Ma one Christmas—all are acquisitions and signs of culture, as necessary to the Ingalls' conception of house as hearth, table, chairs, and bed. Now the family has chosen to leave this particular house behind, taking with them only what they cannot duplicate (tables, chairs and beds can always be re-fashioned), and the *idea* of a house.

And so begins the narrator's tutelage in the terrors and pleasures of open space. Travelling in that endless circle of the plain she perceives that "all around the wagon there was nothing but empty space" (*Little House on the Prairie*, p. 7), that "the stillness seemed dark and empty" (p. 18), that "on the whole enormous prairie there was no sign that any other human being had ever been there" (p. 40). Yet even here, on the road which is no road, they organize the space by both functional and aesthetically satisfying acts. When they make camp, Pa pulls "all the grass from a large, round space of ground," in order not to risk a prairie fire. This space becomes a type of hearth, with the fire "crackling merrily inside the ring of bare ground" (p. 29).

During the day Ma and the girls improvise practically and "playfully" upon their domestic routines. Free to explore, the girls delight in the variety and multiplicity of prairie life. Unable to capture the elusive gopher, they bring Ma a gift of wild flowers instead. These she arranges artistically on the wagon-step, "to make the camp pretty." Nature can be transformed into culture within limits: animate nature can only be observed and internalized as freedom of spirit, or, at the proper time and with the proper rituals, converted into food. Given this sense of freedom within limits, this unique boundary place between the open and the closed (the girls lie in the grass shaded by the wagon while the ever-resourceful and uncompromising Ma irons dresses on the wagon-seat), Laura feels the felicity of space made intimate:

> All around them, to the very edge of the world, there was nothing but grasses waving in the wind. Far overhead, a few white puffs of cloud sailed in the thin blue air.
>
> Laura was very happy. The wind sang a low, rustling song in the grass. Grasshoppers' rasping quivered up from all the trees in the creek bottoms. But all these sounds made a great, warm, happy silence. Laura had never seen a place she liked so much as this place (p. 49).

Delightful as the intermediary camp may be, the Ingalls must attach themselves to the land more firmly and build a permanent habitation. Near a creek bottom on the high prairie in Kansas, some distance west of the Verdigris River, Pa marks out the space for building the house and establishing the farm. The solidity and permanence of this little house is present at its inception—in the vigor, care and purposefulness with which Pa lays the foundation, and in the clarity of intent that informs the narrative description. Yet the house delights Laura especially at a point when the essential form is clearly established but not completely filled in. When the skeleton roof is in place, and as soon as Pa has cut a "tall hole" for the door, Laura runs inside, there to discover the happy space where two worlds meet:

> Everything was striped there. Stripes of sunshine came thorugh the cracks in the west wall, and stripes of shadow came down from the poles overhead . . . . And through the cracks between the logs she could see stripes of prairie. The sweet smell of the prairie mixed with the sweet smell of cut wood (p. 64).

And when the family moves in, under the canvas wagon-cover become a temporary roof and a quilt covering the door-hole, the moonlight inhabits the house in exactly the same way that the sun had earlier: "Its light made silvery lines in all the cracks on that side of the house. The light poured through a window hole and made a square of soft radiance on the floor" (p. 78). Later Pa will build a puncheon floor and a stone chimney, "embellishments" that Ma considers necessary for civilized life. But for this moment the Ingalls are perfectly at home in the house and on the prairie.

The house that unfolds in the pages of this narrative is the "model" house for all the houses of the series. Through it we understand the essence of "house," and are able to appreciate with Laura the variations and improvisations that delight not only because they are novel, but also because they reinforce the idea that a house is something you carry with you, even within you—a mental order as well as a physical space. From the cave-like sod house in *On the Banks of Plum Creek* to the railroad shanties of *By the Shores of Silver Lake*—"half" houses and the most temporary of dwellings, torn down as soon as the railroad encampment moves on—the Ingalls family keeps re-establishing a continuity of form.

All the houses are shelters and store-houses. They are always "little," even when the physical quarters are relatively spacious, because they must make you feel "snug and safe." Inside them the family works and plays, plays in the most serious of ways, using all the armaments of culture. For in later volumes, during the terrible storms, Ma will distract the girls with structured games, Pa will warm them with a marching song, and the girls will sustain themselves by memorizing and reciting biblical and literary texts. And always it is primarily Pa who functions as shaper and bard, making the space habitable by his singing and playing. In fact, his music becomes a part of the natural order: "The night was full of music, and Laura was sure that part of it came from the great, bright stars swinging so low above the prairie. . . . His voice was like a part of the night and the moonlight and the stillness of the prairie" (*Little House on the Prairie*, pp. 51, 79). This benign integration is never total, however, for in the paragraph following the above quotation Laura hears the long wolf-howl, a repeated signature of that part of the natural order which can never be assimilated or mastered.

The little houses and the activities centered in them and radiating out from them constitute one concrete realization of the underlying inner/outer schema. That unassimilable wolf-howl marks another set of relations in the works that involve opposition and mediation. Throughout the series the Ingalls family develops a code for dealing with the wild animal world, partly through ecological necessity, partly through the kinds of human choices that transcend necessity. Animals are food, but Pa would never shoot a little baby deer, "nor its Ma nor its Pa" (*Little House in the Big Woods*, p. 159). And in the luminous final scene of *Little House on the*

Prairie, Pa tells of how during his moonlit hunting foray he spared a stag, a bear, a doe, and her fawn because they were so perfect in their being. But of course animals can threaten human life as well, and one of the specifications of a house is that it be a kind of magic circle, like the archaic fire, to keep the animals out.

While recognizing the necessary boundaries, the narrator also conveys the shifting of categories that the mind performs when trying to deal with this otherness: a bear has hands like a man; another bear is at first mistaken for a cow; Pa courageously attacks a tree-stump mistaken for a bear and thus discovers the "inner bear;" a panther screams like a woman; the dog Jack is once mistaken for a wolf; and wolves look and behave like dogs. At one point in *Little House on the Prairie* the wolves form an uncanny and awesome circle around the transitional house (still with only a quilt for the door). So the house is open not only to sunlight and sweet prairie smells but to the potential dangers of the savage as well. But the wolves, while Pa, Laura and Jack keep watch, do not violate the invisible boundary, and thereby demonstrate their own dignity and inviolability.

Wilder establishes one other significant relation between the civilized and the wild: that great, empty space *has* been seen by human eyes, inhabited by another culture. When they leave the Wisconsin woods Pa promises Laura that she shall see a papoose; Laura transforms that promise into a wish to possess a papoose, a desire that makes little sense until the very end of the narrative. Just as in later volumes the family will be confined to the cabin by the raging Dakota blizzard, so near to the end of *Little House on the Prairie* they cower within the little house, paralyzed by the sounds of Indian war drums and war cries. Their Osage benefactor, Soldat du Chene, persuades the warring tribes to disband, and for almost a whole day the Ingalls stand and watch a human line intersect the endless plain: Indian braves, women and children riding away from west to east. Laura finally sees her papoose, and blurts out uncharacteristically, "Oh, I want it! I want it!" Why does she want it? Because "its eyes are so black," because, I think, it represents the inner immensity that is the counterpart of the outer immensity.

But of course Laura can never really possess the papoose and all it stands for: her task is to internalize those qualities of freedom and innocence. Just as the family must relinquish the little house (the land having been re-designated as Indian territory) and move on, so Laura must stand prepared to relinquish total states of being in the process of growing up. For the tendency of the series as a whole is to modulate from the narration of a mythic experience to a "critical" reading of the myth as a cultural sign system.

Thus Laura, as a young woman undergoing the rites of passage into the womanhood of that particular culture, experiences two epiphanic moments, recollected in tranquillity of course, during which she decodes the "meaning" of her experience. In *The Long Winter* (New York: Harper and Row, 1953) the demarcation between inner and outer becomes particularly acute. The blizzard raging outside can literally kill the family; it also seems to have the power to demoralize them, to efface their humanity. "To survive" is reduced to twisting hay into "logs" to make a fire so that Laura and Pa can warm up enough to twist hay to make more logs, and grinding wheat so that Ma can bake a little bread to keep them alive another day so that they can grind more wheat—a life-supporting but dehumanizing cycle.

> The coffee mill's handle ground round and round, it must not stop. It seemed to make her [Laura] part of the whirling winds driving the snow round and round over the earth and in the air, . . . whirling and shrieking at the lonely houses, whirling the snow between them and up to the sky and far away, whirling forever over the endless prairie (*The Long Winter,* p. 254).

But during a particularly brutal April blizzard Laura's father articulates for her the strength of internalization:

> "It can't beat us!" Pa said.
>
> "Can't it, Pa?" Laura asked stupidly.
>
> "No," said Pa. "It's got to quit sometime and we don't. It can't lick us. We won't give up."
>
> Then Laura felt a warmth inside her. It was steady, like a tiny light in the dark, and it burned very low but no winds could make it flicker because it would not give up (p. 311).

The blizzard-force never really threatens Laura again, but once, when she is nearly grown up, she hears its "voice" in the confusion—the non-language—of a ranting revival preacher. She stands apart, unmoved, exercising her critical intelligence: "She looked at Pa and Ma. They were quietly standing and quietly singing, while the dark, wild thing that she had felt was roaring all around them like a blizzard" (*Little Town on the Prairie*, New York: Harper and Row, 1953, p. 278). The mythic space has been internalized, and Laura's education is complete.

Notes

1. Gaston Bachelard, *The Poetics of Space*, translated by Maria Jolas (Boston: Beacon Press, 1969), pp. 183-210.

2. Laura Ingalls Wilder, *By the Shores of Silver Lake* (New York: Harper and Row, 1953), p. 142.

Myth and Paramyth in John R. Milton's *Notes to a Bald Buffalo*

PAUL N. PAVICH

Paul N. Pavich is assistant professor of English at the University of South Dakota. During recent years he has been at work recording myths and legends of the Sioux people.

Anais Nin points out in her work *The Novel of the Future* (New York: Collier, 1968) that writers of fiction must be free to imagine, to utilize fresh, evocative language and to experiment with form. Nin sees the banality of much contemporary literature as stemming from an over-emphasis on realism and a concurrent negativity toward the wellsprings of the unconscious. This neglect of the non-rational side of people has sapped some authors of their power to awaken feelings of wonder or recognition in the reader. Nin stresses the need for poet-novelists who will be affective on the conscious and unconscious levels with fictions which show the eternal and the everyday in vivid, imaginative ways. In the conclusion of her work Nin says, "Poetry is the alchemy which teaches us to convert ordinary materials into gold. Poetry, which is our relation to the senses, enables us to retain a living relationship to all things. It is the quickest means of transportation to reach dimensions above or beyond the traps set by the so-called realists" (p. 199).

John R. Milton's *Notes to a Bald Buffalo* is an example of the movement toward the type of novel which Nin champions. Lyrical language and imaginative handling of place are essential to the work. Likewise, Milton is not bound by concern for a traditional style and form. *Notes* is a free-flowing set of stories and philosophical insights which reaches toward those other dimensions to which Nin refers. On the first page of his preface Milton explains his novelistic approach with a quote from Eugene Jolas: "I suggest the paramyth as the successor to the form known heretofore as the short story or *nouvelle*. I conceive it as a kind of epic wonder tale giving an organic synthesis of the individual and universal unconscious."[1] Although Milton chooses to call this work a novel, he warns the reader to allow for the dream, the poem and the mystery. It is clear by the end of the novel that his creation is very much in keeping with Jolas' definition of paramyth.

Notes to a Bald Buffalo encompasses generations of Americans: settlers and Indians, cowboys and miners, artists and historians. Each section of the work adds to the totality of the mosaic of times, places and characters. Descriptions of the West blend with myths of the Sioux, mystical experiences, and surrealistic passages. The effect of the novel is an impression of the cycle of lives within the greater cycle of life. The book offers vignettes of many characters' daily lives; yet the reader perceives these glimpses *sub specie aeternitatis*. This correlation of the two aspects of life are exactly what Jolas foresees for future fiction when he says, "The literature of the future will tend towards the presentation of the spirit inherent in the magic tale and poetry, towards the poet's exploration of heretofore hidden strata of the human personality. It will probably express the irruption of the supernatural, the phantastic, the eternal, into quotidian life."[2]

In approaching the magical side of life Milton has utilized an acknowledged fragmentation of form. A certain degree of ambiguity seems proper when one is dealing with matters which do not lend themselves easily to rational, sequential discussion. However, the various parts of the novel ultimately work together toward a unified, coherent impression. Although Milton joins other contemporary writers in experimentation and fragmentation, he differs from many of them in that he does not imply meaninglessness or randomness. The novel is pervaded with an atmosphere of respect for the mysterious creative force of the universe revealed in manifold ways.

Notes is broken down into three sections termed simply beginnings, middles, and endings. Within these sections are grouped brief glimpses of a number of characters at different stages in their lives who are all searching for answers or identities. Because the characters are sometimes left nameless, they seem to be even more representative of universal types. The novel's stylistic flexibility allows for the depiction of the many potential variations and combinations of lives. Within the three sections of the novel there is a certain chronology to the people's lives, but the work reflects what Joseph Frank calls spatialized form. Frank discusses this movement in "Spatial Form in Modern Literature" from *The Widening Gyre*. After discussing a number of modern writers he concludes, "All these writers ideally intend the reader to apprehend their work spatially, in a moment of time, rather than as a sequence."[3] Milton's *Notes to a Bald Buffalo* approximates this description in that it resembles a large tapestry with many stories and time sequences enmeshed to give a single image of lives and experiences.

The various episodes of Milton's novel are symbolically combined by the union of a man and a woman on the beach in the last section. The scene hints at a number of meanings which further show the richness of the total picture. The union could be the coming to terms of contemporary American society and the land, the archetypal expression of the masculine and feminine in all human beings, and the beginning of a new cycle on another level of human consciousness. Adding to the holistic implications of the ending are the internal links which connect the episodes. The land itself is the greatest connector in the novel. Throughout the work the relationship of the people to the land is highlighted as an integrating and eternal process. The characters are formed by their attitudes toward their environment; the poet, grandmother, historian, Indian girl and black rider are all affected by it. This device is an example of Frank's reflexive reference in which the reader remembers a number of allusions which ultimately unite all the pieces of the work.

From the very beginning the land is recognized as a catalyst for connection with the deepest parts of the human psyche. In the "Beginnings" section a couple's drive on the desert causes this reflection: "The real meaning of the land was not in the looking but in the feeling one had for it. It was a land of visions, and the visions came from deep inside each person, not from the things he looked at. The outside landscape provided the conditions, the context, the stimulus for the vision, but it could not bring the vision itself" (*Notes*, p. 15). In the next chapter of the novel the mysterious black rider, who seems to be from a much earlier time than the couple on the desert, has a similar experience in the high plateau country: "He looked for the turnoff, but the blackness surrounded him so tightly that it squeezed his mind, forced his images inward, deeper than they had ever gone before, into a recess of his being that he did not know about, a recess nevertheless crowded with dreams perhaps not his, nor immediate, but old" (*Notes*, p. 17). The land, then, is the constant which binds together the disparate elements of people's lives and makes them part of a greater whole. Not all accept this bond readily; some are destroyed while others join with the endless flow.

Notes to a Bald Buffalo is further enriched by the skillful inter-twining of a number of mythic images and archetypal situations which combine to create a more intensive focus on the relationship of land and people. An image of change and changelessness which Milton uses in the beginning of the book is that of the mandala. In the third chapter of the "Beginnings" section a person on a train is moved to consider the similarity of the land to a great wheel: "Each time the train crossed an intersection of road or fence the lines were pulled out at right angles to the curving horizon like spokes in a huge mythical wheel, the world turning on a natural circle with man-made supports. And yet it was not clear that the wheel turned" (*Notes*, p. 11). The symbolism refers to the eternal, the unitative view of reality. The individual's conception of the wheel is representative of the universal urge toward unity and a sense of place. Milton again centers our attention on the inter-connectedness of man and his environment. The "mythical wheel" corresponds to the idea of the Indian and Tibetan circles which Carl Jung investigated. Jung felt that mandalas were archetypes of wholeness which gave man a sense of belonging. In a discussion of the use of mandala imagery by some of his patients Jung states, "The severe pattern imposed by a circular image of this kind compensates the disorder and confusion of the psychic state—namely, through the construction of a central point to which everything is related. . . . This is evidently an attempt at self-healing on the part of Nature, which does not spring from conscious reflection but from an instinctive impulse."[4] Milton's earth mandala is a perfect combination of two of the ingredients of paramyth that he mentions in the preface: the vision and the region.

Another image of the cyclic movement of the universe is drawn from a Lakota myth. The symbol of the buffalo present during all eternity but now aging is the source of the book's title. At the end of *Notes* Milton refers to the creature's role in the four parts of the cycle of life: "For the buffalo born at the beginning of rock has lost much of his hair and has lost three legs, one to rock, one to bow, and one to fire, and he stumbles badly on the fourth leg and is nearly bald" (*Notes,* p. 126). According to Black Elk's account recorded by Joseph Epes Brown, when the buffalo becomes totally bald and legless the waters cover the earth and the age ends. A new, fresh cycle begins and, presumably, a regenerated buffalo takes up its place. What is interesting about the use of this symbol is that it represents the entirety of creation. Brown notes, "The buffalo was to the Sioux the most important of all four-legged animals for it supplied their food, their clothing and even their houses, which were made from the tanned hides. Because the buffalo contained all these things within himself, and for many other reasons, he was naturally the symbol of the universe, the totality of all manifested forms."[5] By employing this image at the very end of his narrative Milton allows it to function as both a conclusion and the promise of renewed beginnings.

The buffalo image is used again in the middle section of the novel as a symbol of the connection of humanity and history. A woman explains to a poet who is viewing a statue of a buffalo that the animal signifies a number of things: the simplicity of earlier life on the prairie and the bounty of the earth as it cares for its dependents. When the poet playfully taps the testicles of the animal, the woman reprimands him for his lack of understanding. She explains that the buffalo and the plains share a sacredness that is too often mocked or overlooked by contemporary man. The woman's sense of the sacred in the presence of the buffalo is a manifestation of her continued sharing in the basic life-sustaining force of the universe. Her realization connects her with the protectors of life in all ages.

Many of the women in *Notes to a Bald Buffalo* function as teachers for those who need to be reminded of their proper place in the natural order. Char, a young historian, strives to show her skeptical fiance the importance of a sense of history. She assumes an oracular role as she urges him to try to understand the past through the experience of the desert environment. Their story is threaded throughout the entire novel and shows the young doubter's attempt at coming to terms with history and ultimately with a truth that transcends history. An anti-thesis is set up between the man and woman. He stands for the acceptance of only the coldly logical while she accepts a much larger view that includes the intuitive and the mystical. By the end of *Notes* the man has had a brief instant of illumination on a mesa. Throughout the book he has referred to the dust of the earth, but only in the final section does he see that there is any connection between himself and it. A peacefulness settles over him as he understands that he is an integral part of all that exists or has existed in the past or will exist in the future: "He was grateful for his kinship, for his understanding that when he died he would join a great company, his dust sifting in time into their dust, all of the same soil, the same rock, the same sky. It was a comforting thought" (*Notes*, p. 116). The man has admitted his role in the landscape in which he lives, and this has brought him a moment of wholeness.

This character has had what Abraham Maslow terms a peak experience. Maslow mentions a number of attributes which apply to the case of the man on the mesa: a feeling of universality, self-forgetfulness, acceptance, fulfillment. Char's fiance experiences the unitative consciousness which Maslow defines as "a sense of the sacred glimpsed *in* and *through* the particular instance of the momentary, the secular, the worldly."[6] Moreover, the man has been comforted by the knowledge that death is natural and not a cause for fear and anxiety. The integration of the self and the abiding earth is basic to the fabric of the entire novel, but here it is especially powerful. As he approaches Char's home he knows that he has been exposed to something wonderful, a truth which brought him inner calm and a feeling of timelessness. He is like a neophyte returning to his spiritual mentor to discuss his recent encounter with history and the land. However, he is not able to articulate his experience to her: "He knew that something had happened to him on the mesa, something climactic in scope and intensity, but there were no details, no pegs on which to hang the experience, nothing to justify the epiphany. It was gone. Back to the dust. He could not remember" (*Notes*, p. 119). While Char is able to retain her sustaining vision of life's continuum, her fiance again falls into his former mode of thinking. In his concern only for the moment he effectively cuts himself off from the vital meaning of his experience and it fades away.

The instance of Char and her doubting fiance is only one of the many concatenated episodes which illuminate the convergence of the rational and mystical realms. *Notes to a Bald Buffalo* is a move in the direction of the individualized "dreaming forth" of the subconscious world which Joseph Campbell feels is necessary in contemporary society. Campbell thinks that writers must try to connect themselves with the psychological bases which gave power and health to traditional cultures whether medieval Christian, American Indian or Tibetan Buddhist. At the same time he warns against an acceptance only of archaic myths which are not appropriate to modern life. Milton has chosen to incorporate images and symbols of the past with his own insights into humanity to come up with a work that both reaches backward to origins and looks forward to potentialities. By drawing on mythic resources Milton makes the connection between the singular and the universal. Campbell refers to this quality when he says of myths, "They are telling us in picture language of powers of the psyche to be recognized and integrated in our lives, powers that have been common to the human spirit forever and which represent that wisdom of the species by which man has weathered the milleniums."[7]

On the final page of the novel the many layers of myths and visions, beginnings and endings are woven together. The cyclic nature of reality is stressed as the author states, "What is begun must be concluded. This is not a platitude but a word to be taken seriously. And what is concluded must be begun again. We come and we go. This motion is life. On the beach, Wana agli un and he" (*Notes*, p. 125). Milton describes existence as a never-ending cycle, but he is not negative in this assessment of things. The very last line of the work refers to the scene in which the man and woman on the beach are transfigured in a moment of mystical and sensuous union. They are representative of the characters throughout the novel who seek some meaning and find it in other people and in a radical relationship to the land. The man has crossed the continent to have his epiphany with the mysterious woman. His search is over. The Lakota phrase in the final sentence implies that he has come home.

Notes

1. John R. Milton, *Notes to a Bald Buffalo* (Vermillion, South Dakota: Spirit Mound Press, 1976), preface.
2. Eugene Jolas, ed., *Transition Workshop* (New York: Vanguard Press, 1949), p. 29.
3. Joseph Frank, *The Widening Gyre* (New Brunswick: Rutgers Univ. Press, 1973), p. 9.
4. Carl Jung, *The Archetypes and the Collective Unconscious* (New York: Pantheon Books, 1959), p. 388.
5. Black Elk, *The Sacred Pipe*, ed. and recorded by Joseph Epes Brown (Norman: Univ. of Oklahoma Press, 1953), p. 6.
6. Abraham Maslow, *Religions, Values and Peak Experiences* (Columbus: Ohio State Univ. Press, 1964), p. 68.
7. Joseph Campbell, *Myths to Live By* (New York: Bantam Books, 1972), p. 13.

Manfred and Calvin College

PETER OPPEWALL

Peter Oppewall is professor of English at Calvin College, Grand Rapids, Michigan.

Although increasing attention is being paid these days to the writings of Frederick Manfred, one significant period of his life and work is still being neglected. I refer to the years of 1930-1945, which form a basis for his highly autobiographical trilogy, *World's Wanderer.*[1] I propose to take a close look at the four years from 1930-1934 which he spent at Calvin College, and which he chronicled minutely in *The Primitive*. After a brief account of the highlights of his career at Calvin, we shall see what he has made of these events in *The Primitive*. We must also note some of the highlights of his visits to the campus since then because they will help to reveal his reactions to his alma mater and Calvin's reception of her famous native son.

College years are often the most crucial in the intellectual and spiritual development of a young person. Even though the trilogy has been judged inferior to his earlier work and especially to his western novels, I believe that a close analysis of *The Primitive* can yield psychological and spiritual insights useful for an understanding of Manfred's life and work.

Since Manfred's parents were members of the Christian Reformed Church, a denomination whose members are strongly committed to religious education, he was sent to Doon Christian elementary school, and to Western Academy in Hull, Iowa. It was only natural that he should go on to Calvin College in Grand Rapids, Michigan, for it was and is the only college owned and operated by the Christian Reformed Church.

Manfred's treatment of his four years at Calvin in *The Primitive* is a minutely chronicled, intensely personal testament of 460 pages, replete with characters and events that are drawn directly from his personal experiences there. I propose to describe some of these events and influences, paying attention not only to real characters and incidents, but to his imaginative transmutation of them as found in the 1949 edition of *The Primitive*. Manfred himself prefers the more tightly edited and controlled version in *Wanderlust*, but for our purposes the original edition is much more revealing.

Manfred's basic strategy as a writer is to ground himself squarely upon the real world, whether that of his own experience in the autobiographical works, or historical and legendary events as found in the Buckskin tales. The same technique is found in *The Primitive*. Much of his material is remarkably faithful to real events. Other material is based on characters or events that have been heightened or transformed. Still others have no basis in his experience at Calvin. It is particularly revealing to note his inventions or shifts in emphasis because they usually enhance the development of certain themes.

The external events of Manfred's four years at Calvin College can be summarized briefly. After spending two years on the farm in Doon, Iowa, following high school, he came to Calvin in the fall of 1930. The trip east was made in a decrepit Model T Ford, owned by another student who filled it with Calvin-bound students. Several of these became characters in the novel, and at least one has remained a life-long friend. The trip is told in such lively detail that it takes Manfred 78 pages to get Thurs, his hero, to Grand Rapids. He found quarters in the dormitory, or Rooster Brooder as it was called. The first summer he went back to Iowa; the rest he worked on Calvin's campus and lived in an apartment house off campus with fellow students.

Manfred decided early that he would major in English, eventually taking a total of nine courses. He also took eight courses in philosophy, five in history, four in German, and the required five two-hour courses in religion. He followed the teacher preparation program, including practice teaching.

Although he had not played basketball in high school (his home was remote from the school, and he was needed on the farm for chores), the coach was sufficiently impressed with his six-foot nine-inch size to invite Manfred to take up the sport. Applying characteristic determination and enthusiasm, he developed rapidly as a player. *Chimes* (March 20, 1931), the student newspaper, reported at the end of the first season, "The Calvin Freshmen, with Feikema leading the scoring, dropped only two games of a nine-game schedule." He was the starting center for the next three years. By his junior year he was good enough to lead the first team to consecutive successful seasons, a rarity in those days.

But Manfred hankered much more for literary than athletic fame. He began publishing poetry, sketches, and stories in the *Chimes*, the first poem appearing already in his freshman year. By the second year he was invited to join the actively ambitious literary club; by his junior year he was president. Under his leadership the club studied writers like Arnold, Barrie, Galsworthy, Ibsen, Tolstoy, and T. S. Eliot. The same year he became literary editor of the college newspaper. The last year he was associate editor, and also became a member of the intellectually elite Plato

Club. Each year an increasing number of his literary contributions found their way into the *Chimes* and the literary section of the *Prism*, the college annual.

The account of these and other events in *The Primitive* reveals much about Manfred's intellectual and emotional development. The novel appears to be faithful to the spirit of these events and even to Manfred's reaction to them. He comes closest to real life in the physical setting of the scene. He obviously wants to ground the novel on the bedrock of hard facts, a tendency noticeable in most of his fiction. The hardest facts used, though, are relatively unimportant things like the street names in Grand Rapids and the physical makeup of the Calvin buildings and campus. The physical location of most of the activity in the novel can be precisely determined. The trip from Iowa to Grand Rapids can be traced on the map, since he lists nearly every city, town, and hamlet along the way. Any movement within the city is reported street by actual street. Churches, parks, lakes, cemeteries, and other landmarks are faithfully described. The attentive reader can become familiar with much of the area surrounding the college, and the down-town area as well, including Commerce Street, the aptly named headquarters for prostitution of that day. The dormitory is described almost in its entirety with loving detail. The chapel, located in the main building and scene of many campus activities, gets special attention, as do other rooms and classrooms. Manfred even includes the statue of Moses, whose adventures would fill a large volume if they could ever be collected, which stood at the entrance to the chapel. The library, the seminary building, and the grounds themselves sometimes get the same minute attention.

Manfred is also precise in the title and number of the various courses he took at Calvin. He lists them at the beginning of every semester, and faithfully reports his grades at the end, amazingly enough almost always the actual grades he got in those courses. One break in the pattern occurs when his hero, Thurs, switches from English, Manfred's major, to music. Manfred says he made the change because music was a preoccupation of his at the time he wrote *The Primitive*, and he now feels that he could as well have been a composer as a novelist. The switch may also have been made to increase Thurs' frustration and isolation. In actuality Manfred got a reasonable degree of recognition for his literary efforts; the hero of the novel gets none at all for his musical gifts.

Manfred's use of names in *The Primitive* is peculiarly inconsistent. The city is changed from Grand Rapids to "Zion," and the college from Calvin to "Christian." The college newspaper becomes *Cymbal* instead of *Chimes*, and the annual, *Testament* in place of *Prism*. These no doubt add to the religious atmosphere of the college. Yet "Pierian" remains as the name for the literary club and "Plato" for the philosophy club. More peculiar still is his handling of leading writers of the day. Thurs complains that they are neglected in the college literary classes and so reads them on his own or introduces them to the literary club. But they are disguised by such names as O'Never for O'Neill, Sindare Fearless for Sinclair Lewis, Maemy Growll for Amy Lowell, Ida Sweet-Accent Ilay for Edna St. Vincent Millay, Oiler Rollwagon for O. E. Rolvaag, Fitz Shot Hiswad for F. Scott Fitzgerald, B. S. Idiom for T. S. Eliot, and others. Since the disguise is so thin, he may have been merely playing games.

Some of the same kind of name disguising goes on in his choice of the professors' names at Christian College. His motive may have been to protect those who were portrayed unflatteringly from recognition. But those familiar with the college of that or a later day can easily identify them. Manfred's method of naming them is to take letters from either the first or last name and transpose them to the other name: history professor Peter *Hoe*kstra becomes *Hoe*xum Picker, German professor Al*bert*us Broene becomes Lub*bert*us Dornbush, psychology professor *J*ohannes Broene becomes Henry *J*erome, Johanna *Ti*mmer becomes *Ti*llie Krak, Coach *Cornel*isse becomes *Cornel*ius Williams. Similar techniques are followed with some of the student names: John *De* Bie is portrayed as *De*ddes Murreman, John *Huize*nga as *Huse* Starring, *He*len Reitsema as *He*ro Bernlef, etc. Manfred claims to pay very close attention to naming his characters; this may very well be true of his later work, but his patterns in *The Primitive* seem eccentric. He uses first names like Kempis, Spinoza, Erasmus, Nommel, Eevo, Theobaldus, Ingersoll; and last names like Snortebull, Manx-Hamberg, and Sourcole. Apparently he wanted to get away from the obviously Dutch names that predominate to this day on the Calvin campus, and so only a half-dozen remain. As Cornelius Ter Maat has pointed out in his doctoral dissertation *Three Novelists and a Community* (Univ. of Michigan, 1962), the best study of Manfred's relationship to his religious origins, the names sound more Scandinavian than Dutch. Actually they are quite a mixture, with a fair number being distinctly English. Manfred himself has contended that the peculiar names result from an attempt to impart a Frisian flavor to the background. However, there is hardly a distinctively or typically Frisian name in the whole book apart from the one on the cover.[2] In the revised edition Manfred has Anglicized most of the peculiar names. This solution seems a logical outgrowth of his rejection of a distinctive ethnic background in the first edition.

A significant theme in the novel is Thurs' discovery of the importance of his own name and of his Frisian origins. One of the few college professors in the novel definitely *not* drawn on a Calvin prototype is a militantly chauvinistic Frisian English professor, Landric Bernlef. He contends that because of early Frisian settlements in England and some similarities between Old

Frisian and Anglo-Saxon, the Frisians are really more English than the English. That Manfred takes all this seriously can be demonstrated by his novel *This is the Year* (1947), which contains a six-page glossary of Frisian terms, as well as some Frisian history. As a Frisian who grew up among Hollanders who were trying to become Americanized, Manfred has always been painfully aware that he was a member of a minority within a minority. Perhaps he really wanted to establish his credentials with a larger group, much closer to the original settlers of the country, so that he could more legitimately identify with the kind of indigenous materials that have helped to make his recent writing so successful. In order to establish English origins, he has exaggerated the difference between the Frisians and the Dutch, as well as the Frisian influence on the history and language of Engand. It may well be that this same drive was part of his motivation for changing his name.

One of the most significant things we can learn about Manfred's attitudes from *The Primitive* is that while he had ambivalent feelings toward the college, he developed rather consistently negative reactions to the established church. His presentation of the professors and the courses they taught is often very sympathetic, and his respect for the academic quality of the school is high; but the closer he gets to institutionalized religion, whether in the form of denominational politics, church or chapel worship services, administration of the college (note his portrait of the college president, who happened to be a minister and an important denominational leader), or even to some of the students who were studying for the ministry, the more harsh and unsympathetic the portrayal becomes.

The warmest and most accurate presentation of a professor in the book is that of William Harry Jellema, chairman of the Philosophy Department for many years, and one of the most inspiring and influential teachers in Calvin's history. Manfred had eight courses with him and liked him so much that he made him one of the two people to whom *The Primitive* is dedicated. He is labeled early in the novel as "the truest Christian he [Thurs] had ever known" (p. 188).

Other clearly identifiable professors whom he respected were A. E. Broene of modern languages, J. Broene of psychology, Hoekstra of history, and Registrar Dekker. His basketball coach, William Cornelisse, is warmly portrayed. Henry Van Zyl, his practice teaching supervisor, and H. J. Van Andel, from whom he had a course in art, are recognizable.

Some of the less flattering portraits are of Johanna Timmer (Miss Tillie Krak), who actually taught him Freshman English and probably is the one who made him .repeat the course, but who is presented as a zoology professor, and the college president, the Reverend R. B. Kuiper (Rev. Bogardus Cee), who is handled as roughly as anyone on the faculty. He preaches the first sermon heard by Thurs in Zion, and it breathes enough fire and brimstone to invite comparisons with "Sinners in the Hands of an Angry God." The service itself contains both a public excommunication and a couple being forced to stand before the congregation to confess the sin of adultery—ceremonies rarely done in public by that time in Grand Rapids churches, though they may have been more common in the Iowa churches which Manfred attended as a youth. It is also President Cee who takes Thurs to task when his Plato club paper is thought to contain heresy, and he is the one in the novel who sets out after Jellema's (Renold Hobbe's) scalp. Yet even he has a kindly side. In one actual event faithfully recorded in the novel, Thurs and his friends steal fruit from the dormitory kitchen in protest against the meager Sunday evening fare. President Cee invites the suspected but unconfessed culprits to his home for a social visit during which he and his wife serve them basket upon basket of fruit, after which the boys agree, "Theologian or not, the Prex is one hell of a swell fellow" (p. 250).

In spite of the heavy reliance on actual characters for the faculty, two of the most important thematic figures in the novel are modeled on men that Manfred met elsewhere. Broer Menfrid, the music professor, is supposed to have some of Joseph Warren Beach in him. Manfred actually had no music courses at Calvin; yet his hero switches from an English to a music major in his junior year. Manfred needed a different prototype, even though he knew and liked Seymour Swets, the actual music professor at Calvin. Since Thurs is an orphan (again not true to life), Manfred used Menfrid to develop the theme of a search for a father. He befriends Thurs and encourages his efforts to compose music. In volume three of the trilogy, Menfrid turns out to be his real father. The presence of such sustained themes is the most convincing evidence we have that Manfred is right in the contention that the trilogy must be read as a whole and that the publishers did him a disservice by forcing the early publication of *The Primitive* and issuing the volumes separately.

Professor Bernlef, who supplies the Frisian motif, is the other major character change in the novel. The actual English professor, from whom Manfred had possibly as many as eight different courses, was Jacob Vanden Bosch. Manfred must have had compelling reasons for giving up Vanden Bosch, who was surely one of the ablest, most colorful, and eccentric professors on the campus. He could have presented Vanden Bosch with more taste and humor than did another of his students, David Cornel DeJong, who flayed him mercilessly in *Belly Fulla Straw*.

Manfred's heavy reliance on actual people is also found in his presentation of students in the novel. It is safe to venture that most of the students had an actual prototype, though some of the minor ones may be composites, and a rare few, like Willem Sourcole, appear too ludicrous to have much basis in life. A classmate and life-long friend of Manfred's, John De

Bie, who recently retired from Calvin's history department, appears in the novel as Deddes, his dormitory and summer co-worker. De Bie testifies that the events in which he participated are, with some exaggeration here and there, accurately described. In spite of the heavy criticism of religion in the novel, we find Deddes described as "a practicing Christian" and "the kind of goodhearted Christian who made up for the pompous Alexander Paul" (p. 28). Thurs' closest friend, Huse Starring, is also drawn from life, but he in contrast is hypercritical of Christianity and is suspected by President Cee of having drawn Thurs away from the faith.

The way in which Manfred uses actual events, as well as background detail and characters, yet heightens them with his imagination and great story-telling ability, can be demonstrated by comparing a few actual events as told in *The Primitive* with the originals. The famous (at least at the college) hazing scene in which Thurs' back is swabbed with red paint by upperclassmen, and then he is left in the dark marooned with several other freshmen in the attic of the skeleton seminary building, is presented basically the way it happened. But the building was actually almost complete rather than a skeleton. Also, Manfred, by John De Bie's recollection, was not tied. In the novel he bursts the ropes with brute strength and rescues the rest. Thus the adventure becomes more dangerous and more dramatic in the novel and Thurs comes off the hero. The Soup Bowl battle between freshmen and sophomores is described very much as it was apt to happen in those days, but in the novel Thurs holds off most of the sophomore class single-handedly—rather unlikely in spite of his size and strength. The frosh-soph party in his sophomore year *was* actually held at the country club, a most unusual location, and partners *were* chosen by lot as told in the novel. The scene in which a student on a bet runs naked across the campus at night and then to his surprise is exposed by a specially installed spotlight actually happened. Supposedly there is a snapshot to prove it. There really was a student who used expressions like "Egeeberkam," "Frigallility," and "You frickin aye." The last one became so popular on campus it survived to a later generation. The Iowa farm boy who saw the letters P. C. in the sky and came to Calvin to Preach Christ, only to conclude when he flunked out that they really meant "Plow Corn" was a story widely believed, but every generation of students had its own likely candidate. The mock election in 1932 was actually held, and there was campaigning on campus for Socialist candidate Norman Thomas. The results as reported by *Chimes* were Hoover 230, Thomas 115, and Roosevelt 15. Considering the conservative background of most of the students, 115 votes for the Socialist candidate in a student body of 387 was remarkable in itself. Manfred makes it even more dramatic, but less believable, by reporting the results as Socialists 230, Democrats 100, and Republicans 45. He does this not only to emphasize the eloquence of his friend Huse, but to make more plausible the later investigation by the church of conditions at the college.

Although *The Primitive* has been criticized as being episodic and too much like a documentary, it does have clearly identifiable and sustained major themes. These, too, arise naturally out of Manfred's experience at Calvin College. One of the most prominent and consistent themes in the whole trilogy is Thurs' search for the ideal woman. He finds her in the lovely Hero Bernlef, daughter of the unsympathetic English professor. In real life her first name was Helen, and she is the Helen of Troy to whom the book is dedicated along with Professor Jellema. Manfred has her living on Troy Street when she actually lived on Virginia—possibly the only street switch in the entire novel. She was a classmate of his for four years. His passionate and increasingly hopeless love for her seems as honestly moving and sincerely portrayed as anything in the novel. The mortification and ridicule he experienced from his friends over the great discrepancy in their size was very real. Many of the incidents in the courtship are presented as they happened. Her sister recalls the details of the hot chocolate spilling on his lap because of nervousness on one of his earliest visits. The breaking up of another date by the boorish interference of his friends is authentic. The two were fellow members of the Pierian Club for three years; he was president the third year, and she followed him in that position the fourth, just as described in the novel. On the other hand, some of the incidents are exaggerated or fabricated. Although there was a spring Pierian picnic on the beach at Lake Michigan (apparently an annual event) he did not save her life by rescuing her from drowning. The scene in which he shakes her violently and injures her severely shortly before leaving Calvin for good also did not occur. The romance cooled in real life after the first couple of years because of lack of interest on her part rather than the hostility of her parents. Yet he was convinced that he was doomed to fail with her because of physical incompatibility as well as his own clumsiness. It is difficult to exaggerate how much he romanticizes and idealizes her image; he goes so far as to say that "he felt he owed his life to the dream of Hero, if not to the real Hero" (pp. 415-416). Even the revised edition of the trilogy in 1962 is once again partially dedicated to her.

The most persistent and pervasive theme, however, of which the Hero theme is only a reflection, is Thurs' sense of isolation, of separation from his fellow men. Making Thurs an orphan obviously heightens that theme. The hero's feeling that he is different is attributed first of all to his size, but eventually it has psychological, social, and even spiritual implications. This theme is perhaps the most intensely personal and deeply felt of the novel for Manfred, though the circumstances which contributed to it are heightened in the novel as compared to real life. Thurs is literally obsessed with his size; it affects all his relationships with people. Even strangers he meets invariably comment on it. His friends ridicule him constantly, calling him names like "behemoth" and "Dinny" for dinosaur, just as they did Manfred. His friends found it incongruous that such a hulking brute of a fellow should aspire to write poetry. Ironically his size and strength can be put to good advantage, as in the hazing incident, the Soup Bowl contest, fights he is forced into, and especially on the basketball court. But his hero takes little comfort or pleasure in these things, and Manfred deliberately plays down Thurs' success on the basketball court, especially the last two years when he contributed the most and must have become a campus hero. The only game described in his whole senior year is the one in which Thurs goes berserk after an intolerable amount of taunting and dirty play from the opposition. This incident is immediately followed by the epic drunk, which is in turn followed by his running away from school, all of which he feels leave him in disgrace and cause him to contemplate suicide. Thurs' reactions to adversity are often extreme—he sometimes feels that he is "abnormal" or a "monstrosity," and even goes so far as to suggest that he is not human.

Manfred may have been as painfully embarrassed by his humble farm origins as his conspicuous size. To him Calvin College and Grand Rapids appeared as a cultured, sophisticated environment which made him feel like "a freak from the farm." Thurs greatly envies the ease with which some of his friends move about socially and is particularly in awe of the social graces and superior intellectual achievements of Hero. Thurs even claims his high school preparation was greatly inferior to his classmates'. Here Manfred has departed from reality in order to heighten Thurs' isolation; he himself defends the quality of his own high school training, and a faculty study of that time shows that graduates from Western Academy carried the second highest GPA of the five feeder Christian high schools.

Manfred uses shifts in point of view, which are infrequent in the book, mainly to emphasize Thurs' peculiar differences from others. His switches to Huse and to Hero on a couple of occasions are made mainly to give their impressions of Thurs. They emphasize two things—his being a "misfit" or a "primitive," and his great talent or promise for the future. Huse says, "Poor Thurs. All human life, all its habits, its mores was against him. . . . [He was] . . . an 'odd' man lifted up out of a culture that often killed off its 'odd' ones" (p. 265). But he also says that "most of mankind wanted nothing of geniuses" (p. 265). Hero sees him as "a misfit if there ever was one," but she also sees him as having "deep brains" compared to "surface brains," and finds him gentle on one side, but "hard," "unmoved," almost "primitive" on the other side (p. 356). In spite of all the personal defeats and suffering, Manfred wishes to suggest somehow that Thurs has promise for the future.

It is likely that Manfred's honesty in the novel extends to his expression of the hero's religious doubts and struggles, which no doubt increased his sense of not belonging. Hardly a dozen pages go by in this lengthy novel without the raising of some religious concern or question. Although Manfred uses Thurs' friend Huse for some of the severest criticism of the church, he himself (it would seem) becomes increasingly disillusioned and unable to believe in the kind of God which some of his fellow students worship. Actually Thurs wavers between a kind of despair, which says there is no God, and moments of hope like the one during his singing of Handel's *Messiah*: "It was all music of a God, and it almost made Thurs think kindly of Christianity again" (p. 380). After the denomination has dismissed his beloved Professor Menfrid, he decides to resign his church membership. He concludes dramatically at this point, "That does it. Now it comes to me. Everything is sin with them. Everything. And the result is they chase love away. . . . They have system, organization, edifices, but no natural love. Neither of brotherhood nor of sex. They have everything but the heart" (p. 444). Actually it was Professor Jellema who was under fire for his teaching methods at this time, and who did in fact leave Calvin for Indiana University the next year (1935), not to return until 1948. Manfred's separation from the church was not that dramatic, however; he went to church very little during his last two years, but retained his membership in the Eastern Avenue Church throughout his college career.

It may well be that Thurs' considered opinion about organized religion is consistent with Manfred's; at least it appears to be similar to what he has developed in other novels. Thurs concludes that it is "safer to trust the senses and the instincts than the intellect" (p. 409), and that it is better to "live for the sake of man and not God" (p. 293).

In view of the rather consistent critique of the church and many of the things it stood for, it is not surprising that the appearance of *The Primitive* in 1949 caused a stir on the Calvin campus and perhaps somewhat throughout the denomination. Some of the contents may have raised a few ecclesiastical hackles. The book opens with a poetic description of the process of evolution. The very first church service emphasizes the supposedly Puritanical and unforgiving side of Calvinism. The novel treats lightly visits to houses of prostitution, contains a nude dancing scene, and describes several drinking bouts, all presumably by Calvin students. Movie attendance (at that time an issue in the church) is encouraged, and chapel and Sabbath worship spoken of disparagingly. Many of the students are shown to be narrow, rigid, unforgiving people with a mind-set like President Cee. In one scene Thurs suggests to the Plato Club that Christ may have been a homosexual and that Mary invented the notion of the virgin birth to cover up an illegitimate pregnancy. It would be a mistake, however, to focus on these things as primary reasons for disappointment with Manfred's work. The open-minded reader must agree with Manfred's own assessment that he did not set out as an antagonist of his community. After all, he does make attempts to disguise it, however clumsy. His primary concern was not the college. The novel is much more the story of Manfred's own personal struggles and attempts to find himself as an individual. The point of view used reflects almost exclusively Thurs' own consciousness. As Manfred has pointed out, Thurs is not the great hero who succeeds in showing how wrong everyone else is. In fact, in the original version of the trilogy he comes to a tragic end. What is more, Thurs himself says at the end of *The Primitive* as he leaves town, "Christian's all right. It's just that I don't fit in it" (p. 457).

The biggest disappointment to readers of the church and college is that Manfred clearly missed or was unsympathetic to the main purpose for the college's existence. It is supported by loyal church members who hope that their children will be strengthened in their faith and in their commitment to Christ as well as made better informed about the historical and theological significance of Calvinism. Clearly Manfred's faith was weakened rather than strengthened while he was at Calvin. At the college today there is still a certain sadness that he has not moved any closer to evangelical Christianity in his personal religious commitment. Manfred's own religious philosophy may be easier to categorize on the basis of some of his other fiction. A colleague of mine, Peter De Boer, has described Manfred's religion as "spiritual naturalism," defining this further as "looking to nature—land and people—for his values," or finding the "spiritual in the natural."[3] Manfred replied that he was uncomfortable with the rubric, but that nevertheless "maybe De Boer is right."[4] John Timmerman has written that "Manfred seems to be seeking roots in a primitive past, in a sort of mystical appreciation of the continuity and consanguinity of man and nature."[5] Strains of Manfred's early commitment to a love of nature, land and people can be found in *The Primitive*, but not as important themes. Thurs is still looking for a faith to hold on to at the end of the novel and continues this search in the rest of the trilogy.

There is still another disappointment with Manfred which used to come up frequently when his name was discussed at Calvin. Many are disappointed that he found it necessary to change his name. Frisians are perhaps most offended: Why would anyone who claimed to be proud of his Frisian ancestry willingly part with such a mellifluous and obviously Frisian name as Feike Feikema? Then to claim that this original was only a pen name! Many Dutch names are more difficult to pronounce than Feikema, but those proud of their Dutch roots suffer without complaint. Manfred claims that other Dutch families are changing their names.

There is a tendency to Americanize the spelling and pronunciation, but after observing thousands of Dutch names come through the college for the past two decades, I must conclude there is little or no drastic dropping of an obviously Dutch for an obviously English name. I am sure this disloyalty on Manfred's part has now been long forgiven, though at first many found it difficult to call him anything but Feikema. Now the name of Manfred rolls easily from the tongue, but he is still Feike to his old college friends. There is of course an understanding that a national figure has a special need for an easily remembered name, and his many well-wishers at Calvin are pleased with the success of his work that did follow the name change.

There is indeed on Calvin's campus today a large reservoir of good will toward Frederick Manfred. It has been swelled by Manfred's courtly refusal to criticize the school further and to praise it generously upon occasion. In 1963 he wrote to the *Reformed Journal* (May-June, p. 24), "She was a dear Mother. I didn't always agree with her, but I loved her." But the most abundant supply of good will has been built up by his personal appearances on campus. All who have met him are charmed by his justly famed warmth of personality and sense of humor. Professor John Timmerman, a fellow student of Manfred's and a veteran of more than thirty years teaching in Calvin's English department, has said, "I never met a student or faculty member who did not admire and like him, though not all were in agreement with his esthetic or philosophic convictions."[6]

Manfred himself seemed at one time to be unaware of this reservoir of good will on tap at Calvin. He claims that before his success he was treated with coldness by the faculty, and that he was reluctant to return for fear of being regarded as a "monster" or "Benedict Arnold." Yet he has repeatedly come back to the campus at Homecoming time and been very warmly received. His most dramatic appearance was in 1959. It is described in detail in one of his interviews with John Milton.[7] Even though he came unannounced, word got around, and soon he was addressing the whole student body in the chapel auditorium. The response was overwhelmingly favorable. All the aisles were jammed and the audience overflowed on to the platform. Things went very much as described in the Milton interview, including the spontaneous cancelling of classes. Manfred appears to have been deeply moved by the reception, so much so that he could not sleep for the next two nights. Since then he has returned more frequently, attending Homecoming in 1965, 1972, and 1977. In 1972 he spoke twice and drew an audience estimated at 400 in the Fine Arts Center, probably the largest audience to hear a formal lecture by a writer at Calvin. In 1977 he again appeared unannounced, but was invited to speak to several classes. He must have been pleased to discover that two of his novels were required reading that semester in one of the literature courses.

In spite of the recent competition from two very young Calvin writers of national fame, William Brashler, author of *The Bingo Long Travelling All-Stars and Motor Kings*, and Paul Schrader, writer of *Taxi Driver*, and the long established reputations of Peter DeVries, David Cornel DeJong, and Meindert De Jong, most Calvin students, and all Calvin faculty are, I believe, very much aware of and very proud of the reputation and achievements of one of her most famous sons.

Notes

1. Published first as *The Primitive*, 1949; *The Brother*, 1950; and *The Giant*, 1951; but revised, reduced in size, and published as *Wanderlust* in 1962.
2. Manfred was still publishing under his original name Feikema, with his actual nickname Feike as a first name when *The Primitive* came out.
3. "Frederick Feikema Manfred: Spiritual Naturalist," *Reformed Journal*, April, 1963, pp. 19-23.
4. *Reformed Journal*, May-June, 1963, p. 24.
5. "Siouxland and Suburbia," *Reformed Journal*, October, 1959, p. 11.
6. "As I knew Them," *Calvin College Dialogue*, April, 1975, p. 22.
7. *Conversations with Frederick Manfred* (Salt Lake City: Univ. of Utah Press, 1974), pp. 168-170.

Manfred, Neihardt, and Hugh Glass: Variations on an American Epic

ANTHONY ARTHUR

Anthony Arthur, associate professor of English at California State College, Northridge, has recently published a paper entitled "Fremont Meets DeVoto" in San Jose Studies.

When I first started looking into the story of Hugh Glass I thought the question to be answered was this: what is there about it that should attract the attention of two of our most noted western writers, John G. Neihardt and Frederick Manfred? On reflection, though, it seemed that the proper question should rather be: why hasn't this most dramatic of true-life stories been the subject of many more re-tellings? For indeed the saga of Hugh Glass is one of the most compelling adventures in our history, worthy of comparison for what it signifies about the American experience and character with *Moby-Dick, Huckleberry Finn*, and *The Great Gatsby*.

Lest this association with the recognized touchstones of our literature seem overblown, I would add that my immediate purpose is simply to point out that like Melville, Twain, and Fitzgerald, Neihardt and Manfred chose to tell a story that fulfilled, as do these other stories to varying degrees, the essential requirement of the epic: namely, that it offer a definition of the national character, through the depiction of a protagonist whose adventures illustrate and exemplify it. Given the validity of this assumption, I suggest that an examination of the Hugh Glass story as told in Neihardt's *Song of Hugh Glass* and Manfred's *Lord Grizzly* will provide valuable insights into both western American history and the literature that derives from it.

The outline of the story which Neihardt and Manfred adapted is simple enough. Hugh Glass, a hunter with the Ashley fur-trading party traveling up the Missouri River in 1823, went hunting alone and was severely mauled by a grizzly bear. Other members of the party arrived in time to kill the bear and the cubs she had been protecting, but Hugh's injuries were, all agreed, clearly mortal. As the hostile Arikaree Indians were in the vicinity, it was impossible for Ashley's party to remain with Hugh, and he was too severely injured to move, even if it appeared that he could have recovered. Two members of the party were assigned to stay with Hugh until he died, at which time they were to bury him and rejoin the main group. Hugh refused to die, although it still appeared that he certainly must, so after five days his companions left him alone, taking with them his gun, knife, steel and flint. Despite his age—mid-fifties—and his injuries, Hugh regained consciousness after another day or two and proceeded to crawl on his hands and knees, trailing his broken leg, to Fort Kiowa, one hundred miles away. Vowing revenge upon his two companions for their treachery, he then followed and confronted them both and, to his own and everyone else's surprise, did not kill them.

These are the facts of the story. Obviously it has compelling elements on two levels: as a survival tale it belongs, especially for those of us who find it difficult to imagine jogging one mile let alone crawling one hundred, in Ripley's *Believe It or Not.* The mind scrambles for superlatives to describe such a feat and settles, weakly, for "heroic." Survival stories were not uncommon at this time, however, and it is important to note that Hugh's story is different in degree but not in kind from those of Jim Clyman, Tom Fitzpatrick, and Jim Dutton, all of which are recounted in *Lord Grizzly*. Thus, if one of the requirements of an epic is that it be unique in terms of the people it portrays, the fight and the crawl are not of themselves sufficient to make Hugh's story an epic.

What distinguishes it from others like it are the elements of trust, betrayal, and forgiveness. These are differences not of degree but of kind from the other stories, and they do make Hugh's story unique. Both Neihardt and Manfred offer versions which describe Hugh's physical ordeal as a metaphor for spiritual crisis; the differences between their accounts are many but the most important are those of form—in particular, style—characterization, and theme. All of these may be discussed as they are reflected by three key incidents common to both versions: the fight with the bear, the encounter with the old Indian woman, and the confrontations with the wayward companions.

I. The fight. Neihardt tells the incident through the eyes of "a rakehell lad, called Little Jim, Jamie or Petit Jacques" (*The Song of Hugh Glass,* in *A Cycle of The West*, New York: Macmillan, 1961, p. 130) for whom Hugh had a father's love, and to whom is given the dangerous task of luring the enraged bear away from the prostrate Hugh. He maneuvers his horse by the river so that,

> . . . Sliddering in the sand,
> The bear shot past. And suddenly the Grand
> Loomed up beneath and rose to meet the pair
> That rode a moment upon empty air,

Then smote the water in a shower of spray.
And when again the slowly ebbing day
Came back to them, a-drip from nose to flank
The steed was scrambling up the further bank,
And Jamie saw across the narrow stream,
Like some vague shape of fury in a dream,
The checked beast ramping at the water's rim (*Song*, p. 140).

Safe on the opposite bank, Jamie shoots the bear and returns to aid Hugh. Here is the end of Manfred's description of the fight:

> Her massive ruffed neck humped up in a striking curve. Then her head dug down at him. She seized his whole head in her red jaws and lifted him off his feet.
>
> Hugh got in one more lunging thrust. His knife sank in all the way up to the haft directly over the heart.
>
> He felt her dogteeth crunch into his skull. She shook him by the head like a dog might shake a doll. His body dangled. His neck cracked. . . .
>
> Raging, blood spouting from a score of wounds, she picked him up again, this time by his game leg, and shook him violently, shook him until his leg popped in its hip socket. She roared while she gnawed. . . .
>
> Snarling, still spouting blood on all sides, coughing blood, she picked him up again, this time by the rump. She tore out a hunk the size of a buffalo boss and tossed it over her shoulder toward the brown cubs. . . .
>
> The next thing he knew she had fallen on him and lay deadheavy over his hips and legs (*Lord Grizzly*, New York: Signet, 1964, pp. 94-95).

Concerning these versions of the fight, we may note the obvious differences of point of view and of style. Niehardt alternates between omniscient and third-person limited, and tells the opening and closing sections of his story primarily from Jamie's perspective, indicating that the *Song* is as much Jamie's story as it is Hugh's. Neihardt's style is of course dictated by his decision not merely to suggest but to write an epic, as indicated in his foreward. The three stories of which Hugh's is one occupied him for twenty-nine years, and reflected a pattern of "discovery, exploration, and settlement" that was like the other "great epic periods that marked the advance of the Indo-European peoples out of Asia and across Europe." One can only admire Neihardt's fidelity to the form he chose, but the end result is not, to my mind, successful. Although occasional passages are vivid and there are many excellent lines and images, the imposition of a form so alien to this kind of American experience would be quixotic even if it were perfectly done, and Neihardt too frequently lapses into poesy. For example, here is a sunset:

> The sunset reared a luminous phantom spire
> That, crumbling, sifted ashes down the sky (*Song*, p. 138)

And here is a departing flock of crows:

> What augury in orniscopic words
> Did yon swart sibyls in the morning scrawl? (*Song*, p. 202)

Manfred has made the better choice both of point of view and of style, operating from within the mind and body of Hugh Glass so completely as to thoroughly efface himself as creator. Readers familiar with Manfred's other work will recall that vivid action sequences are one of his strengths: I think of Pier Frixen's fall from the windmill in *The Chokecherry Tree*, the runaway truck in *Wanderlust*, or the final scene with the doomed stallion in *Conquering Horse*. In addition to his natural aptitude for suspenseful action, Manfred also brought to *Lord Grizzly* a thorough immersion in the manners and ways of the mountain men, a process described very well in Jacque Pruett's master's thesis on the novel.[1]

The contrasting effect of Neihardt's and Manfred's different methods is readily apparent in the way they deal with the bear. In Neihardt the bear is no more than a plot device to initiate the action. But in Manfred the bear is the dominant symbol of the book, as James Austin, John Milton, and Mrs. Pruett have amply shown. It is sufficient for our purposes here simply to note that for Manfred the bear is not only an animal but Hugh's alter-ego, a symbol of majesty and might, a totem, that, god-like, is both the giver and taker of life; Neihardt's Hugh remains apart from the bear, just as Neihardt, through his omniscient point of view and his archaic style, remains apart from his character. Manfred's Hugh survives by literally getting inside the skin of his antagonist, using its hide, meat, and claws to keep him alive, just as Manfred himself figuratively gets inside Hugh's skin. To pursue the epic analogies and comparisons, Neihardt's Hugh is to his bear as Theseus is to the minotaur and as Odysseus is to the Cyclops, entirely separate; Manfred's Hugh is to the grizzly as Ahab is to Moby Dick and as Ike McCaslin is to his bear, taking his energy and his identity from his enemy.

II. The woman. In both versions Hugh resists the opportunity to help himself at the expense of an aged Indian woman. Considering the circumstances not only of his situation but of the Indian hostilities which have occupied the immediate past, his forbearance is admirable indeed. In Neihardt the encounter is brief, Hugh's virtue is passive—he merely refrains from robbing her—and the significance is explicitly Christian. When the woman appears, Hugh is tempted to rob the "poor crone," for

> What did the dying with the means of life
> That thus the fit-to-live should suffer lack? (*Song*, p. 207).

But he resists as

> Far down a moment's cleavage in the gloom
> Of backward years Hugh saw her now—nor saw
> The little burden and the feeble squaw,
> But someone sitting haloed like a saint
> Beside a hearth long cold. . . . (*Song*, p. 207).

If Neihardt's brief passage is a poetic image, Manfred's is a short story, a dramatic set piece the conclusion to which—the burial—Manfred labored over in his revisions. It is worth quoting at length for what it tells us about the relation in *Lord Grizzly* between setting and theme:

> That night, after the filling moon had come out, with all the land in a silver shine, Hugh with his bare hands dug out a grave for her in the sand bar and held a brief but decent paleface service. He mumbled a few words from Job over her. "Man that is born of a woman is of a few days and full of trouble. He cometh forth like a flower, and is cut down; he fleeth also as a shadow, and continueth not." As an afterthought Hugh also spoke over her as a good Ree husband might. "Now go, my child, go to the land of souls, go to where many of your friends and relatives are already waiting for you. Do not turn back, but look ahead, and soon you shall find them who love you and who are waiting for you. Go, do not turn back, look ahead, and you shall be happy." Sadly he lowered her into the deep hole he'd dug for her. Waggling his old head at the sad turns of life, he covered her over with sand. Then, also free style, he took a handful of sage and rubbed it up and down his arm for purification against what had killed her (*Lord Grizzly*, pp. 158-159).

Setting in *Lord Grizzly* includes not only the land but those who inhabit it, and one of the most striking aspects of the novel is Hugh's heightened sensitivity to the earth. He hears sounds heard by no other men:

> He heard the itching movement of armored beetles deep in the earth. He heard grasshoppers chewing spears of grass. He heard angleworms squirting up out of their holes and excreting rich crumbles of dirt in the surfaces of the earth (*Lord Grizzly*, p. 117).

By virtue of his circumstances and his own nature, Hugh himself is of the earth. He is therefore akin not only to the bear but to the Indian; although they are his enemies, they are all united in deriving their very being from the land. Thus when Hugh reverently buries the old woman Manfred is careful to have him unite his own heritage, that of the Bible, with that of the Indian, creating something new and perhaps unique from their intermingling.

Neihardt's setting by comparison is a painted diorama, not fundamentally different despite his close knowledge of the land from that of James Fenimore Cooper in *The Prairie.*

If the theme of both versions is that Hugh's crawl is a journey towards self-knowledge, we may use the jargon of the psychologists and say that self-knowledge means the integration of mind, body, and spirit. For Neihardt the spiritual emphasis is paramount; for Manfred the land is the *sine qua non*, as Hugh's integration with the land and those who share it with him are necessary conditions for self-knowledge. The setting which in Neihardt is essentially an obstacle is in Manfred the means; the bear, the Indians, the land in Neihardt are transcended by Hugh, while in Manfred they are subsumed by him.

As for what this episode with the old woman tells us about Hugh's character, the most striking difference between the versions is that Neihardt's Hugh merely refrains from an ignoble action, while Manfred's performs a noble act. The essential passivity of Neihardt's Hugh is a constant in *The Song*, beginning with the fight with the bear, which is given to Jamie, and continuing until the end, when it may be said that Hugh's forgiveness of Jamie is a conscious act of mercy dictated by a religious imperative. Hugh *receives* solace in *The Song*; his quest is a process of becoming worthy to receive it. By comparison, Manfred's Hugh is an active initiator of events, both physically, as when he sets his own leg by propping it in the fork of a tree and pulling the bones into place; intellectually, as when he uses the remains of the bear for his own survival; and morally, when he aids the dying woman. But he never receives the comforting solace that he does in Neihardt.

III. The confrontations. The conclusion of the Hugh Glass story as it really happened is described as follows by Mrs. Pruett:

> After fifteen days, Hugh reached Fort Kiowa, then pushed on to Fort Atkinson where he found that the man he sought was a soldier and thus shielded from his wrath. Unable to do otherwise, Glass received his favorite rifle and such other essentials as would allow him to return to his trade, and thus his anger was evidently appeased (Pruett, p. 44).

As I have found several times in trying to describe Hugh's adventure, and as this account shows, the conclusion of the true story is anti-climactic: "And then he found the rascal and—didn't kill him." Both Neihardt and Manfred interpret this abstention from revenge as stemming from virtue rather than from prohibition, and it is in this regard that both consciously impose their sense of what his story means. Thus the moral question which is at the heart of the matter, and which permits us to consider *The Song* and *Lord Grizzly* as literature, derives from the visions of the writers and not from the event.

This distinction is critical, because both writers attempt to go beyond, and in a sense to refute, the popular cliche of the shootout which dominates so much western writing, particularly that which finds its way into the movies.

Both versions stress the obligations which Hugh's companions owe him and the father-son relationship which is violated by the sons. In Neihardt as in Manfred, there are two companions—Jamie, blond and handsome, is good but weak, while Jules LeBon, swarthy and foreign, is bad but clever, the tempter who persuades Jamie to violate his conscience and his duty. In *Lord Grizzly*, Jamie is Jim Bridger, later the most famous mountain man of them all, and Tom Fitzgerald is the coolly self-interested but by no means vicious older man. The moral questions examined in both versions are also similar: to what degree are the young men culpable for deserting Hugh, and to what degree is he entitled to revenge?

Culpability in both cases is heightened by the "sons'" earlier obligations to Hugh and mitigated by circumstances: Hugh's apparently mortal injuries, and the approaching Indians. Interestingly, both authors credit the less admirable of the son-figures with too much learning. In Neihardt, Jules is motivated originally to stay by money—the suggestion of Judas by the phrase—"the silver's clink," is reinforced by indications of Jules' sophistry, also a characteristic of Judas, as he persuades Jamie with

> A self-educated dialectic strife
> That made absurd all arguments for life.

Jules knew

> Unnumbered tales accordant with the case,
> Each circumstancial as to time and place
> And furnished with a death's head colophon (*Song*, p. 197).

Compare the equivalent passage in *Lord Grizzly*:

> Anybody knew that reading made a puffball lighter in the head. Reading filled the head with excuses on how not to be a man in a fix. On how not to be a brave buck. In a fix a bookman sat down and told over all his ideas afore he got to work and shot his way out of a fix. In a fix a man hadn't ought to have but one idea—and that was how to get out of a pretty fix pronto. Concluded to charge—did so. That was what true mountain men did (*Lord Grizzly*, p. 135).

But the similarity between these passages is misleading. Both writers are describing casuistry, or the concept that circumstances alter moral judgments, but for Neihardt the opposition is between faith and reason and there is no question as to the wrongness of the companions' desertion: they are allegorized as "venality and fright." The penultimate line of *Lord Grizzly*, however, is Hugh's reflection that he has "passed through such a passel of things he don't rightly recollect wrong from right no more" (p. 270). The straightforward "Concluded to charge—did so" is adequate for survival but not for life, in which circumstances alter absolutes.

Accordingly, the failure of the sons for Manfred's Hugh is not religious but secular, not a breach of faith but a violation of the "code," that body of rules which Hugh lives by, as, he trusts, do his friends.

This distinction between the religious and the secular aspects of the two versions is critical because in both Hugh is a solitary man, gruff and secretive about his past. And in both he undergoes a mental and physical ordeal that would destroy most men and survives, alone and unaided. If ever a man was capable of living without the companionship of other men, it was Hugh Glass. He is such a solitary in Neihardt, close only to Jamie and to God; but in Manfred Hugh is clearly, for all his grizzly characteristics, very much a part of a larger group. Nearly the first third of Manfred's novel develops the idea that the mountain men were alone together, surviving in spite of isolation rather than thriving because of it. As the following passage shows, it is terrible to be so isolated:

> The land was clean of green grass and running red meat. The sky above was clean of flying flesh. There was nothing but himself and the twinkling stars above and the rustling dried bunch grass below. He was alone. Solitary. There was only himself to feel sorry for himself. There was only himself to tell him he was himself. Only he knew that he knew. He was alone (*Lord Grizzly*, p. 131).

Because Manfred's Hugh is one of a group the members of which depend on each other so completely, the justification for revenge is much stronger in his mind that it is in Neihardt's version. Although Neihardt says of Hugh that

> . . . hate in him was like a still white bell
> A thing of doom not lightly reconciled (*Song*, p. 130),

his hate is in fact rather easily reconciled. When he finds LeBon he spares him out of contempt: " 'I couldn't kill a pup!' " (*Song*, p. 236). And by the time he finds Jamie, who is blind and dying of remorse, Hugh has been transformed by the priestly robes of a father-confessor into an unambiguous Christ-figure.

In Manfred it is not the deserter but the deserted who is driven nearly mad; and it is not the New Testament spirit of forgiveness that saves Hugh but the Old Testament concept of revenge—"An eye for a tooth and a tooth for an eye," as he recalls it—that turns him into a fanatic and enslaves him. Enslaves him, that is, until he is forced by various circumstances to forgo his revenge.

These circumstances, irrelevant in Neihardt, are social in nature and central for Manfred. The first is that Hugh is not guiltless: years before, he had deserted his wife and their two sons in Pennsylvania, and his guilt has festered in his mind just as the maggots have festered in the unreachable wound on his back left by the bear. It is this memory that restrains Hugh in the fight with Jim: "Who was he to cast the first stone? Who was he that he should gouge out the eyeballs of a lad who could easily have been his son?" (*Lord Grizzly*, p. 205). There is, it should be noted, no blinding epiphany in this scene: Hugh releases his hold with great reluctance, and continues to growl and complain at Jim afterward. But though he has concluded to charge and done so, complexities that bookmen love to deal with have restrained him.

Hugh has not only violated the social laws which hold families together; he has endangered the group of which he is now a part, and to whose code he originally referred for his revenge. That is, he got into trouble in the first place by disobeying orders: having covered up for Jim and Fitz, who had fallen asleep on guard and allowed attacking Indians to kill several of their party, he had been restricted to camp duties. Hugh's pride rejected this restriction and he went hunting by himself, violating not only Ashley's orders but a common-sense rule of all mountain men. His injury thus imposed a duty on Jim and Fitz that should not have been necessary. The code, as Hugh has seen it, turns out to be his alone: Jim and Fitz are sorry that they left Hugh and admit their error in saying he had died, but they are not unmanned by fear, like Jules, or killed by remorse, like Jamie. Nobody except Hugh condemns their desertion or condones his search for revenge, and he is finally forced to "forgive" them both because he recognizes his own guilt and because he is not a grizzly bear but a man among other men, a social animal.

* * *

I have indicated that Neihardt's story is Christian in outline and content. Mrs. Pruett has explicated the religious imagery of *Lord Grizzly* and discusses Hugh as a Christ-figure. When he forgives Jim and Fitz, she says, "it is because his tremendous and stubborn soul is influenced by love; then he chooses to be merciful and to abide by something bigger than his selfish pride" (Pruett, p. 149). This interpretation is, I suggest, more appropriate to Neihardt's Hugh than it is to Manfred's. Consider once again the concluding lines, after Fritz has walked away:

And Hugh added to himself in a low mutter, as he cradled Old Bullthrower in an arm, "Turned tame, this child has. Passed through such a passel of things he don't rightly recollect wrong from right no more."

We boys.
O them haunt companyeros.

The plaintive, elegiac conclusion does not so much suggest triumphant selfdenial and transcendance as it does an acceptance of both life's sorrow and of moral ambiguity.

It may be objected that I initially characterized Neihardt's and Manfred's versions of Hugh's stories as epics, and that while *The Song* is clearly an epic *Lord Grizzly* is more in the nature of an elegy, especially in its conclusion. While I do not want to disparage Neihardt's work, which has its virtues, his vision is essentially a romantic idealization both of American history and of his protagonist, written as Tennyson would have written it, merging Darwin, man, and the higher purpose which he doubts not. Indeed, there are echoes of Darwin in these lines:

> Then came on Hugh the fury of the beast—
> To eat or be eaten! Better so
> To die contending with a living foe,
> Than fight the yielding distance and the lack (*Song*, 197),

and of Tennyson's Ulysses, asking "Why seek to climb the ever-climbing wave," in these:

> . . . Why strive at all?—
> That vacancy about him like a wall,
> Yielding as light, a granite scarp to climb! (*Song*, p. 156)

But Neihardt's epic intent is finally defeated because all questions are resolved by Hugh's religious salvation, which has nothing *per se* to do with the American experience.

Manfred, on the other hand, has created a realistic story which has epic proportions because, in addition to the reasons already noted, it is securely based on the facts of our history and on one of its most striking paradoxes: the mountain man himself. Manfred's conclusion is appropriate not only for the character, Hugh Glass, which he has created, but because the nature and destiny of the mountain man was so intensely ambiguous. Never a free agent, he worked for profitable corporations that sold the furs he made available to the populations he despised and fled. A lover of the land, he opened it to settlers who displaced both him and the Indians he fought but respected. Like Teiresias, Hugh prophesies doom, the destruction of his "hunter's paradise," the coming of the "white queen bees" who with their "tame worker bees" would "build honeycomb towns and cities"—"Ae," he mourns, "the enslavement of both land and men was coming here too" (*Lord Grizzly*, p. 160).

Hugh has come, in the course of Manfred's story, to recognize the claims of social obligations in a way that he had not done before. But more are coming. This, I think, is the essence of the American epic that Manfred has portrayed in *Lord Grizzly*, as the vanishing Eden and the illusion of perfect freedom are replaced by the codicils and restrictions of the social contract.

Notes

1. "A Critical Analysis of *Lord Grizzly*." Master's Thesis Colorado State Univ. 1968.

The Myth of the Isolated Self In Manfred's Siouxland Novels

ROBERT C. WRIGHT

Robert C. Wright is the author of the forthcoming Twayne biography of Manfred. He is professor of English at Mankato State University.

"The myth of the isolated self" is a phrase borrowed from Joyce Carol Oates. She uses it in critical essays on Franz Kafka and D. H. Lawrence to suggest that the typical western hero, the rugged not-to-be-daunted individual self against all other selves, is a myth once believed in but now out of fashion. Western heroes have often been depicted as isolated selves able to function well alone, but western writers also have been uniquely aware of the interdependence of all selves.

Paradoxically, humans are indeed separate and isolated selves, but they are at the same time inexplicably joined together. Much of literature, both East and West, has reminded us that we are as we are, separate and together. However, it would seem that as time flows there appear to be alterations in our perceptions of how we are, so that at one period we tend to move ahead by seeing ourselves as isolated individuals, while at another we can progress only as we feel strongly our communal ties to others.

It is my purpose here to discuss briefly the myth of the isolated self and then to show that in four early Siouxland novels Frederick Manfred has consistently devalued isolation and recognized the importance of natural bonds.

Because our sense of separateness and isolation derives from the rational process of dividing, classifying, or categorizing, whereas our sense of oneness derives from our intuitive knowledge, these opposites are often identified as the rational as opposed to the intuitional ways to understanding. Franz Kafka defined these two kinds of truth as the Tree of Knowledge (active) and The Tree of Life (static), where in the first kind Good separates itself off from Evil, but the second is nothing but Good itself. Kafka sees the first truth as pertaining to the fleeting moment and the second to eternity. In an essay on Kafka, Joyce Carol Oates writes:

> What Kafka calls the truth represented by the Tree of Knowledge is a pragmatic, calculating, operative mode of adapting the environment

> to oneself, initially in order to survive but gradually, in civilization, in order to conquer the environment; to press forward, like Faust, hoping for immortality.[1]

What Kafka calls Good and Evil, Oates says, might just as easily be called self and object, for the self always assumes that it is in possession of what is good and that its environment, in so far as it resists the Good, is Evil. The rational mind tends to separate good and evil. According to Oates, the Renaissance ideal is still powerful and its voice tyrannical:

> It declares: I will, I want, I demand, I think, I am. This voice tells us that we are not quite omnipotent but must act as if we were, pushing out into a world of other people or of nature that will necessarily resist us, that will try to destroy us, and that we must conquer. I will exist has meant only I will impose my will on others. . . .[2]

If indeed at one time the world did have to be conquered, and for this purpose Good and Evil had to be separated into self and object (individual and environment), a different need now seems to be upon us—the need to see ourselves as part of a single process, participating in a single event beyond Good and Evil, "beyond language and never experienced by the mind that invented language" (*New Heaven*, p. 281).

Max Westbrook has recognized in the writing of western authors a sensitivity to this need for oneness and uses the term "sacrality" to identify the theme. He defines "sacrality" as follows:

> Basically, sacrality is a belief in God as energy. The powers which thrive in man and in the universe—the good, the evil, the indifferent—are thought to be the original energies which founded the world. This does not mean that ethical values are lost or that the intellect is deprecated. The emphasis must be placed on energy as primary, as a power more fundamental than ethics and the intellect. Once the primacy of sacred energies is granted, the way is cleared for man to bring into full play his local abilities and county values, his intellect and his ethics. Affirmation consists primarily in the belief that a Godly energy can be touched again, tapped anew, at any time; man does not have to lean on his dry, intellectual reading of a past time when God touched the world of ancient ancestors. The sacred man can find his rough and realistic God of energy in the beauty of a lake, the harsh heat of a desert, the blank and haunting eyes of a fresh-killed deer. This discovery, furthermore, is a literal one: the sacred man does not find a symbol of God; he finds God. He touches the thing itself. If he has the irrational courage to do this, then he can shape primordial energies in ethical directions. If he lacks this courage, the energy remains, but without direction, having only the pent-up and destructive rage of

> power betrayed; and a frustrated energy will break out in distorted actions or even in the final distortion: suicide.[3]

As a contrast to the Renaissance point of view, which glorified the conscious, private, grasping self, consider these words from the closing paragraphs of D. H. Lawrence's *Apocalypse*:

> We ought to dance with rapture that we should be alive and in the flesh, and part of the living, incarnate cosmos. I am part of the sun as my eye is part of me. That I am part of the earth my feet know perfectly, and my blood is part of the sea. My soul knows that I am part of the human race, my soul is an organic part of the great human soul, as my spirit is part of my nation. In my own very self, I am part of my family. There is nothing of me that is alone and absolute except my mind, and we shall find that the mind has no existence by itself, so that my individualism is really an illusion. I am a part of the great whole, and I can never escape. But I can deny my connections, break them, and become a fragment. Then I am wretched.[4]

As a human race, we continue to be fragmented and wretched, largely, as Oates says, because the myth of separate and competitive selves endures, obsessing us with ideas of being superior, of conquering, of destroying. But change is in the air, perhaps has been developing all through this century. In this decade several writers (Arthur Koestler, Rene Dubos, Andres Weil, Thomas Kuhn) have noted the possibilities. Among them is George B. Leonard, who writes in *The Transformation* (New York: Delacorte, 1972), p. 11:

> Actually there is nothing essentially human or natural in our present situation. The illusions of separateness and alienation have been created only by enormous, exhausting efforts. The walls between us and our fellow beings are merely one aspect of the ruins of a dying culture. . . . Perhaps we can sense new beginnings that involve regaining a balance, mending the artificial splits between mind and body, spirit and matter, man and nature, the individual and the social.

A similar note is struck by Theodore Roszak who speaks of the myth of "objective consciousness" which has persuaded us to believe in the reality of nothing that cannot be weighed and measured. "So long as that myth is followed," he writes, "not even the most humanly intentioned among us will find any course to follow but roads that lead deeper into the wasteland." Freed of that myth, though, we are open, Roszak feels, to a new reality through a "wise return to the source from which human culture takes its beginning."[5]

* * *

This return to sources is a motif Manfred has chosen to thread his novels upon, from *The Golden Bowl* to *Milk of Wolves*. The clue may be seen in his use of the "Old Lizard" as an expression of the ultimate source of intuitional knowledge. He explains it this way:

> Our civilization, and all the other levels of nations we have gone through, and all the things we've learned to do by reason and because of common sense, have gradually wiped out our most powerful ally. And that is our primate nature. What I call the Old Lizard. Or the Old Leviathan. . . . It is stronger than the subconscious. The subconscious is a piece of the Lizard. The Lizard is really the primate who is the wisest.[6]

In Manfred's first novel, *The Golden Bowl* (St. Paul: Webb, 1944), Maury, the young tumbleweed on the move, is a good example of an isolated, active self, wary of connections either to people or to the land. Pa Thor, on the other hand, is so closely connected to soil and family that the wrinkles of his skin are identified with those of the dying earth—man and soil are one. From the beginning Maury's isolation is threatened by the need the Thors have for him, and he is aware of the natural pressures working to help him build connections and set down roots. He tells Kirsten a little story:

> "Well, I was tired one day an' I lay down in the grass, an' I saw a thin green worm crawlin' on the end of a blade of grass. I watched it, reachin' an' lookin' an' reachin' fer some place to go. It reached, an' finally . . . I pushed another blade a grass so the worm could reach it. Then it crawled down an' hid in the deep roots."
>
> Kirsten rubbed her legs, looking at him wonderingly.
>
> "Sometimes I gotta feelin' that you people are pushing a blade a grass fer me" (pp. 98-99).

But Maury is not ready to establish roots until he is reborn symbolically from mother earth in the well-digging episode. He is lowered into the earth, is encased in water, and is pulled forth after being cramped into a fetal position. Even though Maury leaves after this episode, his perspective has changed, he seems to have authority over Pa, and he will return. When he does, he thinks, "He had done something terribly wrong. He had, for four years, doubted the land. In the years to come, he would work doubly hard to make the earth, and his own heart, forget that he had been unfaithful." Maury realizes that his earlier view of himself as a wanderer, an isolated self, was a mistake. What happens to Maury is akin to what happens when the self is transcended by participation in an event, as when the Zen disciple realizes that the riddle must be experienced, not as puzzle, but as event. When this happens Maury sees his finite self as part of the infinite, and the "profane," dusty farm, which his reason rejected, now appears to him to be paradise (*New Heaven*, pp. 268-269).

Where Maury is able through denial of self to visualize the dusty South Dakota farm as a potential paradise, Pier Frixen in *This Is The Year* achieves the opposite effect, transforming his farm paradise into hell through his determination to conquer alone. As Joyce Carol Oates says, in discussing Kafka and Lawrence, "The attempt to achieve victory of any kind—even victory over one's own impulses, even victory over the flow of time—is the tragic revision of paradise into hell" (*New Heaven*, p. 270).

In the sense that Pier is a perfect example of one who "overestimates the self to the exclusion of other realms of being," *This Is The Year* (New York:Doubleday, 1947), is a tragedy, at least in the view of a Kafka or a Lawrence. Pier is the typical western hero pitting himself against all other selves and seeing nature as a thing to be conquered, or at least classified and dissected.

When friends try to get Pier to work together with them to improve prices, he refuses, saying, "Fair or not, I'm agin' anybody tellin' me what to do. I'm independent, I am. I run this farm myself. I don't ask nobody about nothin', do as I please, an' am my own boss." A little later during the same conversation he says, " . . . I believe God wants us to work nature to the brim, get what we kin, an' He'll do the rest" (pp. 468-469). Pier has the hero's relentless drive to be first. His father, who has been rudely deprived of his farm by Pier, says to his son, "You'd rather go into debt up to your ears than let somebody get ahead of you. You're worse than a race-crazy trotter" (p. 76).

Pier has contempt for his father (the past) and for Pederson, the county agent (the future), choosing to isolate himself in the present. From his father, Âlde Romke, he could have learned something about cooperation. In reminiscing about the old days, the father says,

> "An', Pier, you a Frisian, an' you don't remember the story of Adel, how he was the first in history to start the wonderful custom of men sharing their kill together? How, after a hunt, he would prepare the guest meal of roasted meat, how, after everybody had eaten, he would make them kiss each other, even them that had bad blood between them?" (p. 265).

But Pier shrugs and says, "I don't care to remember." Neither does Pier care to look ahead to the future by taking care of the soil. Pederson, the Old Dreamer (Lizard), tries to teach him methods of conservation, but Pier never takes the agent's advice. At one point Pederson is so frustrated, he preaches a sermon to the chickens. It is in this sermon that Manfred clarifies the metaphor that has dominated the book—the earth as woman. As in *The Golden Bowl* where Pa Thor resembles the soil, so here Nertha,

Pier's wife, clearly suffers as does the land. Manfred has Pederson say to the chickens:

> Man is born of the earth and the earth is born of man. All the chemicals, all the ingredients, all the parts that are to be found in man's body are to be found in hers.
>
> The soil breathes. Its nostrils are the plants and the trees and the animals and man.
>
> The soil digests. It digests even more efficiently than man's alimentary canal. Throw iron into it, or steel, or even radium, and the old lady will decompose it, or digest it. . . .
>
> Man the fool has been reckless with his wife. He has behaved foolishly on her breasts and her thighs. Here in America he is losing her, will lose her, has already lost half of her (p. 480).

Pier does lose both his farm and his wife through a stubborn need to conquer and destroy. In this early book, Manfred has anticipated the writers of this decade who have been calling for a new kind of heroism.

Just as Manfred characterizes Pier as a bull in his rape of the land and of his wife, so in *The Chokecherry Tree* (New York: Doubleday, 1948), he extends that metaphor to include all the bullying hero-leaders of the world. In Chapter XVI, Manfred, as author, writes a letter for his leading character, Elof Lofblom, to the President of the United States and all other international leaders, addressing them: "Dear Mr. President (and all the above mentioned Horned Bulls)." This letter cautions leaders against destroying the world with the atomic bomb by giving it to our heroes.

Manfred has to step into his story and write the letter for Elof because he has made his hero inarticulate, an insignificant chokecherry tree of a man dominated by towering cottonwoods. In one of the author notes which introduces each chapter, Manfred apologizes for trying the impossible:

> . . . Elof, the only one capable of putting into writing the true pit of yourself is yourself. Yet the moment you become capable of doing so, you are no longer Elof (p. 121).

Even though there is no way for Elof to express himself, Manfred says, "there is no harm in trying the impossible."

Thus Elof, in having diminished intellectual power, is set against the accepted pattern of the western hero who has a dominating, destroying ego. Elof could never be President. He is not a horned bull. Yet his destruction and ours is threatened, Manfred suggests, by the products of the intellect, particularly the atomic bomb. Joyce Carol Oates writes:

> The intellect, a technique of perception and an aid for survival, can evolve too far, can become confused by its own inventions, and must perish, must die out, just as certain animals with extra-ordinarily developed characteristics of specialization must give way to those more suited for adaption to the environment (*New Heaven*, p. 270).

If Elof isn't a hero, he is a survivor. When a landslide covers a truck full of children on a Sunday School picnic, only Elof and his friendly rival live. The minister and Elof's mother see this survival as a sign from God that Elof should be a minister. He is sent to prepare in college but fails, as he fails with women, and as a traveling salesman. In all of these adventures he has sought success, not on his own terms, but for others and in imitation of others. It is when he gives up and returns home that happiness comes to him quite naturally, without his effort or control. This kind of acceptance is not intellectual but is suggestive of the spirit of Taoism, in which, as Oates says, there is "an awareness of a dominion of absolutely impersonal and incomprehensible Being over the efforts of individuals to influence it, or even influence their own lives" (*New Heaven*, pp. 276-277).

In another author comment, Manfred recognizes the shortcomings of pure intellect and the value in qualities Elof represents:

> . . . One thing troubles us. To have survived the numbing discovery that you were a simpleton and not a hero, to have discovered within yourself courage enough to come home to certain abuse and ridicule—could it be that a special quality resides in you after all? That we, pompous and lofty, and warbling with a fancy tongue, are blind to it? That intellect, which we worship just a little more than we fear, and consider our only hope, is as heady a drink as religion? Is as much an Opium? To have survived that double strain is perhaps the true hero's toil. . . . (p. 246).

As in *The Golden Bowl* and *This Is the Year*, Manfred shows in *The Chokecherry Tree* a resemblance between the human and the natural. The last line of the book reads, "Elof, the leaf; Lofblom, the flowered leaf." The true hero may be the one who, as a leaf which falls back to nourish the mother tree, participates within a great coherence and fosters the "going on" Manfred cherishes.

There is good reason to believe that Manfred's understanding of the "great coherence" developed out of his personal struggle to "go on" in spite of a serious bout with tuberculosis, if his autogiographical *Boy Almighty* (St. Paul: Itaska Press, 1945) can serve as evidence. He entered the Glen Lake Sanatorium in April of 1940 and left in March of 1942. *Boy Almighty* is the record of Eric Frey's fight against the disease, but his spiritual health is under treatment as well.

When Eric Frey enters the sanatorium, he is a thoroughly isolated self. Although his communicable disease is a clear demonstration of his interconnectedness with others, he has been living in starving isolation as he writes his first novel in a rented room. In a fashion typical of purely intellectual understanding, he sees himself as a lonely individual at the mercy of "good" and "bad" forces from outside his person. The "good" is the sun, which he finds ennobling. "I crave sunlight. I'm a sunshine boy," he says (p. 253). The "bad" is the Whipper, associated in Eric's mind with his father but also with a punishing supernatural force. "Sometimes I think there is a devil out to do me dirt," he tells his nurse (p. 38). To Dr. Fawkes he explains the Whipper as "something in the universe, a hard hearted God" (p. 102).

Through Eric's participation in the tuberculosis event he comes to a different understanding of the human condition. The helping sun and the punishing Whipper are as much connected to him as are the other patients in the sanatorium, as is his father, who brings a gift of peace. From the kindly and patient Dr. Abraham he learns much about self-discipline, and the need to obey rules for the sake of others. He is especially subdued when he learns that a person may have died because of his own petty quarrel with a nurse. There are interdependencies. He is not an isolated self. He also learns from his roommates Huck Olson and Dr. Fawkes. Where he at first feels superior to them, he learns humility as his own selfishness and arrogance are measured against the irascibility and simple courage of Olson, the gentle wisdom of Fawkes. In mourning Fawkes's death, Eric thinks, "I loved you because you taught me that the Whipper does not exist except in ourselves, and that we find order and chaos just as we choose" (p. 275).

In surrendering his isolation, Eric does not surrender his uniqueness, only his isolation. In *The Book* (New York: Vintage, 1972), p. 71, Alan Watts explains how this can be:

> The point, which can hardly be repeated too often, is that differentiation is not separation. The head and the feet are different, but not separate, and though man is not connected to the universe by exactly the same physical relation as branch to tree or feet to head, he is nonetheless connected—and by physical relations of fascinating complexity.

That the self is a part of a larger reservoir of energy, as suggested in the Max Westbrook definition of sacrality, Manfred seems to have come to understand through his sanatorium experience at the crucial moment when his writing career was to begin.

This paper has considered only Manfred's first four books, published in the 1940's, but the bonding theme informs his entire work. The story of

Hugh Glass in *Lord Grizzly*, for example, is the story of an isolated self coming to terms with "we boys." In *Milk of Wolves* (Boston: Avenue Victor Hugo, 1976), Manfred's most recently published novel, he moves the sculptor Juhl Melander from the isolated self he is in the city to the integrated self he becomes in the wilderness, where he learns to be one with the Indians, the wolves, and the trees. Juhl finds himself one day under the great trees entranced with the organ sounds, trying "to rhue in tune with the master voices of earth." He sees a family of wolves and says, "They. We. We're all in it together" (pp. 185-186).

From the start of his career, then, Manfred has sensed that we are in transition from the perspective of the individual as isolate to that of the individual as an interlocking member with all living things. It is ironical that the perspective of the individual as isolated self was necessary for the conquering and settling of the West, but that the perspective of interdependent selves, relearned from the conquered native Americans, is the view of ourselves that may be necessary to save us from self destruction and to move us along the way.

Notes

1. Joyce Carol Oates, *New Heaven, New Earth* (New York: Vanguard, 1974), pp. 279-280. Hereafter this work will be cited parenthetically as *New Heaven*.
2. Joyce Carol Oates, "A New Heaven and Earth," *Saturday Review*, November 4, 1972, pp. 53-54.
3. Max Westbrook, "The Practical Spirit: Sacrality and the American West," *Western American Literature*, 3, No. 3 (Fall 1968), 198.
4. Harry T. Moore, *D. H. Lawrence: His Life and Works* (New York: Twayne, 1964), p. 267.
5. Theodore Roszak, *Where the Wasteland Ends* (New York: Anchor Books, 1973), p. 422.
6. Frederick Manfred, *Conversations with Frederick Manfred* (Salt Lake City: Univ. of Utah Press, 1974), p. 42.

"The Delegate for Poetry": McGrath as communist Poet

FREDERICK C. STERN

Frederick C. Stern, assistant professor of English at the University of Illinois, Chicago Circle, has for many years admired and studied McGrath's poetry.

Thomas McGrath is a Communist, and sometimes, more recently, a communist poet. That seems to me the beginning of his art, and, if not its end, its crucial component. It is by no means all of his art. But the many other things one might say about him—that he is a modern poet who works in many traditions and forms, that he is a North Dakota-born American poet, that he is a myth-creating poet—all these things are, as it were, modifiers of my first sentence—that McGrath is a Communist or communist poet. His communism places McGrath in a tradition—other aspects of his writing place him as well, but his communism is very important in placing him—just as surely as being a Christian poet places Eliot or being a Beat-hippie poet places Ginsberg.

It is my intention in this essay to deal with McGrath as communist poet. I want to be very careful about this central aspect of his work, however. It is easily misinterpreted, unless at least some of the modifiers of the statement are also understood. It is also easily misunderstood because the term "communist" or such words as "Marxist" or "radical" can mean a variety of things and are no longer, if they ever were, terms for the monolithic ideology which American cold-war years myth created. I propose in this essay, in the main then, to establish that McGrath is a communist poet and to discuss the relationship between his verse and his communism. In doing so, I will necessarily neglect many other important aspects of McGrath's poetry. That I feel free to carry on such a discussion without fear that I may be doing McGrath harm is, perhaps, a sign of our times, a sign made manifest fairly recently by the death of the ignominious congressional committee which cost Thomas McGrath a teaching job in the fifties. Though Watergate was no watershed, things are a little more open for a while, so that I don't think it will cost McGrath another job to be identified as a communist poet.

In what ways, then, is McGrath a Communist, or communist, poet? We can note first that much of his poetry is concerned with the specific language and experience and with events and personalities related to the life of the American Communist Party. In writing about *Letter to an Imaginary Friend*, Parts I & II (Chicago: Swallow, 1962, 1972), McGrath has said that "What difficulties exist in the poem are those of reference (generally not crucial to an understanding of the poem)."[1] But that is only partially true. Some of his references in *Letter* as well as in other poetry are likely to be quite obscure to those who might not know of the specifics of the life of the Communist party of the United States of America, as obscure as, and more so I should think than, are some of, say, Pound's allusions to historical personages.

One or two examples will demonstrate. Most readers of *The Movie at the End of the World* are likely to know who the Angela Davis is to whom "The Rituals of the Chapel Perilous" is dedicated. They are less likely to know that Henry Winston, to whom the poem is also dedicated, is the Black National Chairman of the CPUSA, a man who lost his eyesight while in prison on Smith Act and other charges. Winston's name becomes more important yet because "Two Songs from 'The Hunted Revolutionaries' " is also dedicated to Winston, and these poems appear in the 1964 *New and Selected Works* as "for Harry Winston." There is more involved here than mere "reference" not crucial to understanding. The "Hunted Revolutionaries" songs make best sense when one understands that leaders of the Communist Party had "gone underground" in the early fifties. They were convinced by the pervasiveness of McCarthyism, and especially by their relatively easy convictions during a series of Smith Act trials, that they could not get fair trials—which was certainly true—and convinced that they had to be available outside of prison to their Party and that fascism was a very real and near threat.

These two poems and their dedications, in addition to demonstrating McGrath's involvement with the specifics of Communist Party personalities, both early and late in his work, also show changes in states of feeling about his communism. In the earlier "Song," the conviction of, or at least the hope for, progress of the revolution comes out of the struggle against the repression of the fifties. The later "Chapel Perilous" poem provides for sources of hope in much more personality-embedded feelings. It is the figures of the older revolutionary, Winston, and the younger, exciting, and brilliant Davis, who re-humanize radical politics, gone drab, drear, mechanized in the speaker's view. It is not hope for revolution, but a simpler hope—"the crying became human," "language regained its meaning"—which is here being expressed. I take the last line of the poem to indicate that those attending the "Continuous meeting," having heard the voices of charismatic and humanizing leaders, can now become part of the "popular magic," the on-going political struggles of the sixties, which were not being led by Communists, but by such "new left" forces as SDS.

Examples of the importance of specific reference could easily be multiplied. Many readers will know of Mike Gold, to whom "Men of the Third Millenium" (*Movie*, p. 35) is dedicated. It is less likely that readers will know of some of the other figures of importance in McGrath's poetry who come from Communist Party cultural activities, such as Charles Humboldt: "—and Charlie kept me alive there:/Humbolt: [sic] the warm current" (*Letter*, II, p. 130). Humboldt, who died in 1964, was an editor of *Mainstream* (later to become, for a short time, *Masses & Mainstream*), was earlier an editor of *New Masses*, and eventually became an editor of *The National Guardian*, all journals associated at that time with the Communist Party. Humboldt was a gentle man, highly literate and knowledgeable, something of an "in" legend among Communist and other radical intellectuals in the late forties and fifties.[2]

McGrath's Communism, then, is demonstrable in part because of the direct, frequent references in his verse to figures which come out of the history of the CPUSA and cultural or political groups allied with it.

Places, events, organizations, all play a similar role. McGrath's poetry is frequently involved with the myth that New York's Communist community at times attached to the National Maritime Union. Here was romance, the glory of real proletarians in real struggle, a genuine history of working-class courage in the face of repression. "Showboat" Quinn is easily recognized as a new York NMU leader much admired—apparently rightly so—by the New York left during the earlier forties. But the myth was rather short-lived. After World War II, the NMU held out for some time against the general CIO accommodation to cold-war politics—for some time only, however. Joseph Curran, the NMU president, soon made his peace with the CIO leadership and with the State Department, broke with his erstwhile Communist allies, and did little to support such old-time co-workers as the union's Black secretary, Ferdinand Smith, who was eventually deported to the West Indies. Not long after this break, the NMU moved out of its old, dilapidated West Twenties headquarters and built a fancy, new and plush union hall at about 12th Street. This knowledge is needed to understand McGrath's

And the talking walls had forgotten our names, down at the Front,
Where the seamen fought and the longshoremen struck the great
 ships
In the War of the Poor.
 And the NMU had moved to the deep south
(Below Fourteenth) and built them a kind of Moorish whorehouse
For a hall. And the lads who built that union are gone. (*Letter*, II, p. 123)

Just a few lines later, further enhancing this picture of the labor movement which is so important to McGrath, we read:

> . . . "Business unionism!" says Showboat
> (Quinn). "It certainly do hit the spot with the bosses!
> Backdoor charters and sweetheart contracts—sell out the workers
> And become a by-god proletarian statesman like Sweet Walter.
> Takes a liberal kind of stiff to make labor-fakin' a *pure* art." (*Letter*, II, p. 124)

The "Walter" in question here is probably Walter Reuther, a favorite Communist Party target.[3] The lines further emphasize the poet's sense of loss at the older, militant, pre-cold war tradition of the labor movement. McGrath's references, then, are frequently most accessible to those familiar with American Communist Party history.

Another aspect of McGrath's communist poetry has to do with his use of the specialized language of Marxism. He uses such language, at least as he knew it and often as the American Communist Party used it, in the materials of his verse, perhaps as a teaching device. Thus, one of his earliest published works is entitled "The Dialectics of Love." A poem first appearing in *Figures of the Double World* is entitled "The Uneven Development of the Heart" and echoes the Marxist notion known as the uneven development of capitalism. In "Men of the Third Millenium" we find "Knowledge of Necessity, All-freeing Power," language which echoes a Marxist notion about freedom, articulated by the Russian pre-revolutionary philosopher Georgi Plekhanov as "Freedom is the recognition of necessity." Sometimes McGrath uses such language with humor and even with parodic intent, as when he paraphrases Lenin with "And someone is saying/ 'Sex plus electrification equal socialism' " (*Letter*, I, p. 64).

One could multiply these examples, and one can find them throughout McGrath's work, from his earliest to his latest poetry. McGrath then apparently makes a conscious choice to be a Communist and a communist poet. His use of this often jargony language of Marxists in general and American Communists in particular partly reflects the way he thinks, but also has to do with the teaching function, one which McGrath plays for Marxism, as an Eliot plays it for Christianity—each for their own brand.

A far more important component of McGrath's role as communist poet has to do with the intertwining of political and personal experience in such a way that the reader can come to understand the shaping of the politically engaged personality of the persona of the poems. A case in point is the rather novelistic section III of *Letter*, Part I. The poem recalls the speaker's initiation into the life of work on the farm and the simultaneous initiation into labor struggles. The central figure in that initiation is the farmhand Cal, the young boy's friend and teacher, who is badly beaten by the boy's uncle because of a proposed strike of the traveling farmhands. The strike is lost, the men slink away, and the boy is profoundly upset by the experience. From the dramatic rendering of this past, the poem takes us to the speaker's present, quoting "Showboat" Quinn of the NMU:

And Showboat
Quinn goes by (New York, later) "The fuckin' proletariat
Is in love with its fuckin' chains. How do you put this fuckin'
Strike on a cost-plus basis?" (*Letter*, I, pp. 23-24)

The strike and Cal's beating are intense personal experiences for the boy. They become, in time, part of his developing radicalism, referred to several times later on in the poem to explain the persona's political actions and convictions.

The interaction of personal and political experience is, perhaps, the most pervasive element of *Letter*. Thus, the poem's speaker discusses his father's revolutionary proclivities. He connects the break-up of his marriage to the consumerism of the society in which he lives. In his movement from Communism to communism, we come to understand not only the political sources, but also the profoundly personal implications of such an ideological change. In regard to this change, McGrath quite consciously makes his protagonist's experience, perhaps his own experience, the subject of his poetry when he writes near the end of *Letter*, II:

Ancient Witness
—all unchanged in the time of this poem . . .
All to be changed.
I offer as guide this total myth,
The legend of my life and time. (*Letter*, II, pp. 210-11)

A good deal of McGrath's Communism has about it an anachronistic flavor. His characters often derive more from the Wobbly heritage, which the Communist Party adopted, than any other. This shows in his language sometimes, in the use of such I.W.W. words as "scissorbills" and "bindlestiffs," words which those in the cultural orbit of the CPUSA might still have recognized in the forties and fifties, when they were used in McGrath's poetry, but which would have been quite foreign to most others, except a few older members of the working class which they seek to describe.

McGrath is at times aware of the anachronism of his position, especially in part II of *Letter*, and in some of the later poems in *Movie*, as, for example, in the poem "Something Is Dying Here":

I invoke an image of my strength.
Nothing will come.

Oh—a homing lion perhaps
made entirely of tame bees;
Or the chalice of an old storage battery, loaded
With the rancid electricity of the nineteen thirties
Cloud harps iconographic blood
Rusting in the burnt church of my flesh . . . (*Movie*, p. 182)

It should be clear, then, that in language, in reference and allusion, in political attitude, and in the yoking of personal experience with political experience, McGrath is a poet profoundly influenced by the cultural and political ambience of the Communist Party. But I have said earlier that McGrath is, especially lately, a communist rather than a Communist poet. By that change in capitalization I mean to indicate, of course, his move from the Communist Party of the USA to a more independent—and much more lonely—and personal variety of communism. I cannot date precisely, from his poetry, when McGrath switched from his earlier Communist Party allegiances to become a member of the "unaffiliated far left." Nor are the reasons for his change entirely clear from the verse itself. In a 1975 interview, he described himself politically as follows: "I consider myself a social revolutionary. Always have. I want to revolutionize this whole damned social system and substitute socialism for the mess we've got now. I'm not a Socialist, though. When anyone asks my politics, I tell them, 'Unaffiliated far left.' That act got me canned as professor at Los Angeles State College in the 1950's."[4] What is clear from the poetry is that sometime after his appearance before HUAC there is a change in the persona McGrath has created. "The Committee comes by with its masked performers/," he writes, "To fire you out of your job, but that's expected." Later in the same section of *Letter*, I, however, the image of the lonely, politically isolated person, who will dominate much of *Letter*, part II, makes his appearance. After invoking the figures of Mac and Cal, who along with Showboat Quinn, are the most "proletarian" of the poem, we read:

I turn away then
Unforgetting
Seeing a little piece of the old true unregenerate dark
Extruded into the afternoon classical light—
A little Contra-Terrene matter among the pure shit of the poets—
The world's inescapable evil that we must eat and sing.
And turn away then
From the shop, from the sea,
Toward the desert of the world, the wild garden,
With my politics: to be with the victims and fighters.
(*Letter*, I, pp. 96-97)

It is not till part II of *Letter* that we find clear evidence of McGrath's disenchantment with the political forms revolutionary politics have taken in that new moment. Early in part II, one becomes aware of the increasing sense of loss and of remembered sadness, and of an increasing number of images related to darkness, caverns, graves—images of burial, aloneness, and near-despair. These images are often coupled with a desperate salvation of the political view of the protagonist of the poem, and, one may assume, of course the poet as well:

"Ain't no grabirons a man can lay hand to. *I tell you it's* DARK
DOWN HERE MAN!
slippery dark
can't see
I tell you it's hell—"
We must walk up out of this dark using what charms we have.
Hell's everywhere, this only seems like hell, take my hand,
It is only required to open your eyes—
see
there's
The land as it was
. . . .
Unchanged and changed.
I tell you millions
Are moving.
Pentagon marchers!
Prague May Day locomotives
With flowers in their teeth!
And now the red ball is hammering in—
Spot an empty! Grab an armful of rods!
I'll take you
In the final direction . . .
Only: open your eyes . . .
But it's hard, hard, man.
I'm standing *here*, naked
As a studhorse in a rhubarb patch
Waiting
waiting
and here—
Around me
trouble built for small boys and crazy men!
For my purpose (as I keep saying) is nothing less
Than . . . .

To elaborate the iconic dynamite of the authentic class struggle
In other words to change the world
—Nothing less.
It's hard and I'm
Scared . . .

(*Letter*, II, pp. 107-108) [5]

These lines demonstrate the protagonist's despair at the existing political situation in the country and the world as a whole, as well as on the left. The reference to the Prague May Day locomotive, reminder of the fateful Dubcek period in Czechoslovakia, is crucial. The answer for the protagonist of the poem comes here, as in some other sections of *Letter*, from his personal and individual determination to bring about socialism. While this may be a surprising decision for a former Communist Party adherent, it is not surprising at all for a North Dakota-born and bred American. McGrath's protagonist has shown himself throughout the poem to be a maverick. It is in character, then, that he reverts to a kind of Emersonian self-reliance when the props of the movement with which he was associated are knocked out from under him. The protagonist's fear is a sign of the poet's awareness of the difficulty of "going it alone." He is "scared" not only because the revolutionary task he has set himself is enormous, but also because he is uncertain of his own strength. He is "standing here, *naked*," he says, and in "Something is Dying here" he invokes his strength—but nothing will come.

Thomas McGrath's communism, then, is a little anachronistic, harking back to an earlier day in American radicalism than his present, neither the sophisticated Marxism of the young, the basically unchanged communism of "the Party," nor the spiritual "radicalism" of the "movement" of the sixties. It convinces us of its sincerity and depth. I think it is accurate in its portrayal of the malaise of American life, and it is filled with the righteous anger of an honest man. McGrath's communism must be judged, at least for the purpose of evaluating his poetry, as a vehicle for his art, a framework within which he can build and render the vision of his life. Combined with his love of land, his "outsider" stance, his roots in the American frontier experience, his reversion, when the need arises, to self-reliance, McGrath's politics does for his verse precisely what Eliot's Christianity does for that poet—it provides a framework of conviction and thought and imagery in which he can operate. We need not share fully McGrath's radicalism, any more than we need to share Eliot's Christianity, to appreciate either man's poetry.

Thomas McGrath is the only American poet I know (perhaps Walter Lowenfels is another) who approaches, if not in quality then at least in outlook, the magnificent achievements of such European and Latin

American radical poets as Brecht, MacDiarmid, Neruda and Quasimodo. He is, within the American cultural matrix, indeed our "delegate for poetry."

NOTES

1. Thomas McGrath, "McGrath on McGrath," introd. James Bertolino, *Epoch; A Quarterly of Contemporary Literature*, 22 (1973), 208.

2. Several of the poets whom McGrath mentions, or to whom he dedicates poems of his own, have been included in an anthology, Walter Lowenfels, ed., *Poets of Today: A New American Anthology* (New York: International Publishers, 1964). Among those to whom McGrath gives some prominence and who can be found in Lowenfel's anthology are Charles Humboldt, Don Gordon, Naomi Replansky, and Mel Weisburd. Lowenfels supplies brief biographies of these poets in an appendix.

3. McGrath attacks Reuther elsewhere in *Letter*, e.g., p. 118. The Communist Party's position toward Reuther can be verified in William Z. Foster, *History of the Communist Party of the United States* (New York: International Publishers, 1952), p. 353, et passim.

4. William Childress, "Thomas McGrath," *Poetry Now*, 2, No. 4 (1975), 1.

5. I am grateful to Thomas McGrath for permission to print extensive quotations from *Letter to an Imaginary Friend* and *Movie at the End of the World.*

Robert Bly: The Point Reyes Poems

WILLIAM J. LOCKWOOD

William J. Lockwood, associate professor at the University of Michigan, Flint, has written on poet Ed Dorn in Contemporary Literature (*Winter, 1978*).

In his recent poems Robert Bly seems to wish to tell a story and to share an earned wisdom. Those poems tend to adopt a narrative form—issuing in discoveries or illuminations of the remarkable life in commonplace occasions—a narrative form that seems to be connected with Bly's thoughtful journeyings through the western half of the United States over the last eight or nine years. Now, as Lionel Trilling astutely pointed out in his study *Sincerity and Authenticity* (Cambridge: Harvard Univ. Press, 1971), the art of the narrative as an instrument of holding an audience spellbound and, in the process, of bringing into play feelings of wonder, has fallen into disrepute in modern literature. It has generally come to be viewed as "inauthentic" inasmuch as the narrator of such work appropriates to himself the assumption that life is capable of comprehension. About Bly's own recent work I would raise the question, then: Are these poems "old fashioned" in the sense in which the good old narratives suspended disbelief and attempted to interpret the sound and fury of life in order to make it signify? But so large a question itself must first be more particularly considered since it assumes the validity of the terms of the question and of its applicability to these poems.

We should begin first by asking: Which "narrative" poems? and, also, what journeyings relevant to their composition?

The group of poems that seem to me most representative of Bly's recent work appear in the slim collection called *Point Reyes Poems*. They were written out of Bly's arrival at and extended stay in a particular locality, the peninsula that juts out into the Pacific Ocean about fifty miles north of San Francisco, especially at fairly remote places on that peninsula. First published by a local California small press called Mundra: Half Moon Bay, in 1974, they were reprinted *in toto* as the second part of the three-part volume *The Morning Glory*—and subtitled "Prose Poems"—by Harper and Row a year later. That eight of the ten poems have local Point

Reyes place-names in their titles implies that this Pacific coast location significantly affected Bly's imaginative awareness.

The Point Reyes poems, as they appear in *The Morning Glory* collection, stand, moreover, within a specifically defined American context. The poems in parts one and three indicate travels of discovery through the western half of the continent. "At a Fish Hatchery in Story, Wyoming," "In the Courtyard of the Isleta Mission," "A Poem about Tennessee" (the easternmost poem except for a poem written on the English coast), and "On the Rocks at Maui" (Hawaii, the westernmost poem) indicate the geographical range of Part One. "Going in a Helicopter from Riverside to the L.A. Airport" and "Visiting Thomas Hart and His Wife in Kansas City" in Part Three suggests a more casual and topical range appropriate to the volume's shift of direction, which is homeward, to the Middle Border region, and to its concluding with seven Minnesota "homeland" poems. Of this latter group, the last two poems are what might be termed epiphanies, the one triggered by a Christmas midnight mass and the other prompted by the advent of a New Year's Day. Interestingly, however, these closing poems are laced with references to the sea and to the mysterious undersea life of whales.

The relevance of the Point Reyes poems and of the journeyings which frame them lies in Bly's increased sense of the connectedness of things not only in nature but, to some limited extent, also in history. By virtue of such connectedness the narrative element seems right. From the earlier poems, e.g., in *Silence in Snowy Fields* (New York: Harper, 1962, rev. 1967), one gets the sense that Bly's Minnesota farm was an authentic place largely because of its existential remoteness from the jaded, narrow, fashionable patterns of the Eastern United States, especially its patterns of intellectual and literary pretension; that in rural Minnesota Bly's mind was free to travel to more vital sources of imaginative energy—to Neruda and Vallejo in South America or to Lorca in Spain, for example. His employment of the underground, surreal image, surfacing out of homely, commonplace scenes or occasions, recalled in its intensity the outlook of earlier post-World War II writers who, like Creeley, cultivated the lyric as a force against that which was false.

Many of Bly's recent poems, however, imply, as I have suggested, a stronger sense of continuity, that is, a knowable relationship between how things have come into being and how they began. Now Bly's work has always argued for the continuous elements of existence, but in a Platonic kind of way: they lay beneath consciousness in the authentic unconscious.[1] To put ourselves in touch with that connectedness, we had to turn off the light of intellect and enter into the dark knowledge that the body has managed to store, the otherwise lost consciousness that had been displaced by man's early cutural shift from a matriarchal to a patriarchal order. We had to learn to recognize the authenticity of an essentially feminine consciousness, and in reading Bly's poems this meant allowing ourselves to be surprised into the significance that was revealed in non-logical images. "Matriarchy thinking," Bly wrote in *Sleepers Joining Hands* (New York: Harper, 1973), p. 32, "is intuitive and moves by associative leaps." "And," he added, "it is interested primarily in what is inside walls, unlike patriarchy thinking which tends to regard the linear 'space between the walls.' "

Sleepers Joining Hands seems to have been intended to recapture the lost continuity of feminine consciousness, to restore the balance between a suppressed feminine consciousness and a triumphant masculine consciousness in our nation and in our age. But another opposition seems also to be at work in these poems and it presents itself in the form of a conflict in Bly's writing here, between his allegiance to an authentic mother consciousness, on the one hand, and his need for artistic self-possession and control, on the other. His insistent use of the pronoun "I" and of cumulative rhetorical series appears to have been an attempt to find a form that could successfully include both. Yet the poems did not quite succeed because the urgency to revive feminine consciousness in an increasingly death-oriented society predisposed Bly toward a receptivity at odds with artistic discrimination. Thus he wrote, almost confessionally:

> It is better to forget all that
> and lose yourself in the curved energy.
> I entered that energy one day,
> that is why I have lived alone in old places.[2]

Life in America has indeed been imbalanced in the direction of will and power, and most recently, as the Vietnam experience revealed, death. And yet an indigenous energy characterizes its history, an energy that issues from the dynamics of the pattern of men and women moving through the continent from "the inside walls" of one place to "the inside walls" of another place. It is associated with the masculine principle and it marks the outline of that continuity, or if you will, that series of discontinuities, that marks our history and has been codified in the image of the man journeying West, a journeying not altogether unlike that of Bly himself to a place in which he might discover a substantial correspondent to some aspect of his mind's yearning: for him, Point Reyes, on the westernmost edge of the continent.

"Curved energy," to adopt Bly's own phrase, appears in these Point Reyes poems too. Only here Bly tends to view the forms of the authentic unconscious within a specific geographical and cultural context, that is, in terms of the forms of the land and, though to a far lesser extent, of man's arrival there. Thus in the titles of most of these poems appear place-names that signify the presence of such men: Limantour Dunes, McClure's Beach, Drake's Bay, the Pierce Ranch, and so on.

In "Trespassing on the Pierce Ranch" two sorts of "curved energy" are to be found. One involves Bly's recognition of his divided self as reflected in the image of the pale three-quarters moon moving in daylight, southward, through the clouds:

> It sails eerily forward just as we do . . . I am separated
> from myself as it is from the earth . . . the two go along together.
> Half of me is down here.

But the other sort of energy in this poem consists of Bly's imaginative apprehension of a historical and geographical continuity. That apprehension not merely supplies a frame for the image of the speaker's divided self, but also constitutes a distinct and parallel clarifying motion of mind within the poem, one which begins to define for the speaker an understanding of who he is in relation to where he is in time. As he "walked toward Tomales Point," he quietly realized that "these first sloping lowlands" he saw were those "the Eastern traveller saw as looking over the rail he suddenly came on a continent! In the middle of the endless ocean." And thus his mind began to move inland,beyond those lowlands, to re-create the land forms that these rising coastal forms initiate: "And this is the frail land that thickens out in Nebraska, and the rocks that hold up the heavy pueblos." Bly's insight thus re-creates the experience of the early sea-traveller's linear motion of mind suddenly curving into an awareness of something wholly unexpected and new as he discovered a continent.

Bly's journey and the Pacific seafarer's journey thus made correspondent imply a continuity of experience. For the reader, the correspondence constitutes a wondrous narrative by virtue of which he is led to a clearer sense of his own place and of his own historical identity. Unlike the early poems' leaps of awareness into a mystical realm and the later poems' cumulative moral urgency, the final discovery image is made to stand as a correspondent to a central aspect of the initial dramatic situation. The poem's closing image of a Hopi initiation ceremony, an image of "within walls" feminine consciousness in the history of our continent, refers back to, and has its origins in, the initial related images of the Eastern traveller and of the rock base Bly perceives through his eyes, that which holds up the heavy pueblos the traveller's descendants would later build inland:

> Behind these lowlands the coast range, and behind that Nevada, and behind Nevada the running boys that the old men hit lightly with twigs, their heels hitting the earth drum, as they run toward the dancing ground, that has a stripped cottonwood tree at the center, and a sheep hanging high up on it.

Another way to put this is to say that Bly's recent poems express a more unified sensibility because single images are more satisfactorily sustained. They are sustained not willfully, but in a manner appropriate to a voice unfolding a story full of wonder. And that voice, the "I" of the poems, is relaxed, easy, candid, the final effect of the poems being full and unself-conscious sincerity. Such an effect is singularly evident in Bly's "The Dead Seal near McClure's Beach," and I would like to focus on that poem. But before I do so, I would argue that this is the effect of the collection of all ten poems. The narrative power, strongest in the "dead seal" poem as we shall see, also runs through them.

"Sunday Morning in Tomales Bay," for example, tells of a boat ride out in the bay and of the special effect of it, the sudden disappearance of blue sky and the phenomenon of being surrounded by fog, so that objects in the landscape lose their ordinariness and become strangely beautiful. What seems to be a machine, a derrick, turns out to be alive, to be a great blue heron. The bird is seen to have a timeless and strong beauty that suggests the quality of rare vases or the elegant necks of women in an old Hittite empire. As the story unfolds, we come into the presence of sea-lions who appear to be angels peering at a baby, as though parodying the Nativity. Next, more sea-lions, hundreds of them lying on the shore, and then the heron re-appears, ascending on its long wings. Finally, after the sea-lions have disappeared under the water, a final image of the heron which "flies away thin as a grassblade in the fog." The narrative voice brings us into a marvelous presence, into what Trilling terms a pure "sentiment of being," and it carries us through stages by means of which we are made to sense the continuity of life through time. Interestingly, too, the allusion to the old Hittite empire does not distract us from the sense of place here, a singularly Pacific coast place, but rather intensifies the presentness of it.

"Climbing up Mount Vision with My Little Boy," a narrative of a mountain climb and of father and son's conversation and story-making *en route* is rather too ingenuous, especially in context, but it does exemplify the characteristic drift of these pieces toward a sense of the clarifying wonder of storytelling. "November Day at McClure's Beach" might have been a purely descriptive poem in another poet's hands, but Bly is firmly *in* it, and as he allows the scene to inundate his consciousness, so, through his narrative voice, does it inundate ours:

> The waves smash up the rock, I find flags of seaweed high on the worn top, forty feet up, thrown up overnight, separated water still pooled there, like the black ducks that fly desolate, forlorn and joyful over the seething swells, who never "feel pity for themselves," and "do not lie awake weeping for their sins."

So Bly's voice carries us, in a state of suspended disbelief, toward the conclusion, a new consciousness of floating, of "sailing on skeletal eerie craft over the buoyant ocean."

Donald Hall, in a videotaped interview with Bly, remarked on how Bly's poems often keep moving, discovering new energy in new insights; how one expects the poem to stop but how it keeps pushing on. I think one feels that motion which does not stop and which suggests the continuousness of life in the passage just quoted from "November Day." But that feeling is most powerfully generated in that two-part poem which, with its forty-seven lines, is the longest in the group, "The Dead Seal near McClure's Beach." Here the narrative form, not only the narrative voice, is quite explicit. It begins:

> Walking north toward the point, I come on a dead
> seal. From a few feet away, he looks like a brown
> log. The body is on its back, dead only a few
> hours. I stand and look at him. A quiver in
> the dead flesh. My God he is still alive. A
> shock goes through me, as if a wall of my
> room had fallen away.

The self-indulgence that characterizes Bly's earlier work, justified by a sense of moral or political urgency appears here: "My God he is still alive." But it now appears in the presence of the narrator simply and unselfconsciously allowing himself to stand, naturally, within the story he tells. This presence serves as a means of achieving artistic control—without that artificial sense of distance and objectivity that the poets of the fifties felt so bound to. "This is the oil," the narrator goes on. "Here on its back is the oil that heats our houses so efficiently." An American landscape truly: a California oil-spill. But the poem does not dwell on the implications of this observation. Rather, it goes on, fascinated, noting the scratches on the seal's "old overcoat" skin, scratched by "sharp mussels maybe." And then:

> I reach out and touch him. Suddenly he rears up, turns over.
> He gives three cries, like those from Christmas toys. He lunges toward
> me.

The narrator gradually comes to realize that the dying seal is in a state of consciousness wholly alien to his own. He does not want to be touched by man, does not want to be nudged back into the sea, but wants simply to die. The animal's apparent indifference to life lies deeper, in a desire to be free to swim the wave-like curves of death. And so the poem moves toward a close of simple farewell:

> Goodbye brother, die in the sound of waves, forgive us if we
> have killed you, long live your race, your innertube race, so

> uncomfortable on land, so comfortable in the sea. Be comfortable in death then, where the sand will be out of your nostrils, and you can swim in long loops through the pure death

The effect of Bly's own reading of this poem upon an audience of students at my university last winter struck me as an instance of the power of poetry to hold the listener spellbound, inducing a sense of wonderful self-forgetfulness. On reflection, the poem's effect on this occasion precisely corresponded to the deliberate diminution of the "I" as mediator in the poem's motion toward a close. The narrative voice had set in motion and ultimately yielded place to a web of images and rhythms which could embody that sense of otherness Bly intended.

In the case of Bly's recent poetry, as exemplified in the Point Reyes poems, it seems reasonable again to underscore the apparent connection between, on the one hand, the poet's stronger sense of continuity—thematically, in his attention to place, and aesthetically, in his care in developing single images—and, on the other, his journeying through the western half of this continent. Bly's resistance to the dangerous rigidity and *self*-consciousness of his native (characteristically Scandinavian and Germanic) northern region and his evident sympathy for the open, unselfconscious outlook he seems to have found in the coastal Point Reyes area are no doubt opposite sides of the same coin. Those poems do in any case indicate a promising alteration of emphasis. They generate a moral clarity that is, for the most part, free of pretension to superior wisdom on the part of the telling voice, remaining a process more than an arrangement, forms of illumination more than of judgment, *active presences* into which the reader is drawn and deeply involved. They suggest yet another step in Bly's distinctive career as poet and moral teacher for contemporary America.

Notes

1. I am indebted throughout this paper to Trilling's sustained reflections in *Sincerity and Authenticity*, but especially to Chapter VI, "The Authentic Unconscious," pp. 134-172.
2. From the fourth section of the title poem in *Sleepers Joining Hands*, entitled "Water Drawn Up Into the Head," p. 65.

Willa Cather's Pioneer Women: A Feminist Interpretation

SUSAN ROSOWSKI

Susan Rosowski, assistant professor of English at the University of Nebraska, Omaha, has recently published articles in Studies in English Literature *and in* NOVEL.

Critics have long recognized the pioneer theme characteristic of Willa Cather;[1] yet the significant fact that Cather develops this theme in a manner that runs against the main tradition of American literature has been virtually ignored. Put quite simply, this tradition is a masculine one, and Cather's most forceful pioneers—Alexandra Bergson and Ántonia Shimerda—are women.

Cather's treatment of pioneer women must be interpreted within a context of the general theme common to all her work—the need for an individual to deal with permanent values. For Cather, the ideal human condition involves a synthesis between elements traditionally separated by sexist divisions: the otherworldly, creative, active need for metaphysical "great truths" generally identified with male characters and the worldly, personal, stable values generally represented by female characters.[2] By creating pioneer women who struggle to reconcile these elements, Cather increases thematic tension by placing a character traditionally limited to the personal, worldly, immediate in a context that demands also otherworldly, creative, outgoing activity.

In *O Pioneers!* (Boston: Houghton Mifflin, 1941) both characterization and action present a synthesis between two basic human activities, progression and maintenance. The novel develops in two stages, corresponding to development of these elements in its major character, Alexandra Bergson. In the initial stage, Alexandra moves outward, toward permanent values; in the second, she gets an anchorage of personal stability with which she can maintain permanent value.

The tension between these elements is caught by the novel's first sentence: "One January day, thirty years ago, the little town of Hanover, anchored on a windy Nebraska tableland, was trying not to be blown away" (p. 3). The most fundamental concerns are inescapably present to the early pioneers: human impermanence is everywhere apparent; survival itself is in question. But, such a context also offers the great hope that an individual may develop his or her potential to be fully human by dealing with the universals that are so forcefully present in "the great fact that was the land itself, which seemed to overwhelm the little beginnings of human society that struggled in its sombre wastes" (p. 15).

With this opening, Cather presents the familiar pattern in American fiction of the frontier waiting to be tamed by the noble pioneering spirit. The usual protagonist for struggle is, of course, male. But Cather places a woman, Alexandra Bergson, in this setting and proceeds to demonstrate that *O Pioneers!* will not follow the tendency of novels "to identify the fully human with the male—to see women as flat embodiments of a particular force or theme, to see them mythically, allegorically, symbolically, but never realistically—as fully rounded, complex human beings."[3] When a traveling man admires her hair, Alexandra defiantly rejects becoming an object of his "flirtatious instincts": "She stabbed him with a glance of Amazonian fierceness and drew in her lower lip—most unnecessary severity" (p. 8). Through the "unnecessary severity" of Alexandra's response, Cather makes it clear that her protagonist will not be limited to traditionally feminine roles.

In the first stage of *O Pioneers!*, Alexandra moves towards the universals usually reserved for men. Her progression is made explicit when, on his deathbed, Mr. Bergson passes responsibility for the family to Alexandra, saying "Everything will come on you" (p. 26). Again Cather contrasts this action to the traditional feminine role: "In his daughter, John Bergson recognized the strength of will, and the simple direct way of thinking things out, that had characterized his father in his better days. He would much rather, of course, have seen this likeness in one of his sons, but it was not a question of choice. As he lay there day after day he had to accept the situation as it was, and to be thankful that there was one among his children to whom he could entrust the future of his family and the possibilities of his hard-won land" (p. 24).

Alexandra continues to move outward until, in the famous scene on the Divide, she is "dissolved into something complete and great."[4] Here she transcends the present when "she felt the future stirring" (p. 71) and transcends her material self by joining the universals represented by the land: "The air and the earth are curiously mated and intermingled, as if the one were the breath of the other. You feel in the atmosphere the same tonic, puissant quality that is in the tilth, the same strength and resoluteness" (p. 77).

In subsequent sections of *O Pioneers!*, Cather turns to the second major challenge offered to Alexandra—to maintain permanent values in a complex society. The difficulty of this task is represented clearly. Alexandra is at home on the land: with it, she assumes a creative, traditionally male role. Yet the increasingly complex and artificial society growing around her is antithetical to this primary relationship, for it demands that she conform to a passive, traditionally feminine role. Cather presents Alexandra's brothers and their wives as relatively pure examples of this demand. Their argument over Alexandra's rights to the land is simplistic at best in its dependence upon conventional roles. Oscar and Lou declare, "The property of a family really belongs to the men of the family, no matter about the title. If anything goes wrong, it's the men that are held responsible" (p. 169).

Faced with an increasingly stratified society, Alexandra must do more than reject the roles others impose upon themselves and upon her. She must also forge an individual, personal life through which she can protect the pioneer ideals represented by the land. The challenge she faces is offered by Emil when he declares, "Alexandra's never been in love, you crazy! . . . She wouldn't know how to go about it. The idea!" (p. 154).

Cather answers this challenge in the Marie-Emil and Alexandra-Carl actions. In the former, Cather focuses on a danger implicit in the rhetoric of modern society which holds that the way to permanent value is through romantic love. Marie Tovesky is a supremely attractive character. Like Alexandra, Marie is courageous and strong willed; unlike Alexandra, she is sensitively imaginative in her personal relationships. Despite this potential, Marie's development is almost symmetrically inverse to that of Alexandra. Alexandra is portrayed through a progressively expansive movement; Marie is portrayed through a progressively restrictive movement. The conception underlying each is evident in her initial description. Alexandra was presented as defiantly rejecting the traditional feminine role imposed upon her by the drummer; Marie is presented in a grotesque parody of the conventional love courtship ritual. When Marie's uncle takes her to the marketplace, "His cronies formed a circle about him, admiring and teasing the little girl, who took their jokes with great good nature. They were all delighted with her, for they seldom saw so pretty and carefully nurtured a child. They told her that she must choose one of them for a sweetheart, and each began pressing his suit and offering her bribes; candy, and little pigs, and spotted calves. She looked archly into the big, brown, mustached faces, smelling of spirits and tobacco, then she ran her tiny forefinger delicately over Joe's bristly chin and said, 'Here is my sweetheart' " (p. 12).

This introductory scene foreshadows the later development of Marie. Conventionally, she falls in love and, in defiance of her uncle, marries the dashing, handsome Frank Shabata. But for Cather, romantic love is by definition limiting. It insists that the lovers look only to each other for value: even Emil asks of Marie, "*Why* had she ever run away with Frank Shabata, and how could she go on laughing and working and taking an interest in things. Why did she like so many people. . . . Why did she care about any one but him?" (p. 179). And Frank, perversely feeling that his happiness would result from Marie's unhappiness, thinks, "If he could once have made Marie thoroughly unhappy, he might have relented and raised her from the dust. But she had never humbled herself" (pp. 221-222). In Cather's novels, the outcome of romantic passion is inevitably unfortunate: lovers who attempt to live according to the conventions of romantic love gradually lose that love, as in the marriage of Marie and Frank. Or, by the romantic outcome of death, lovers escape the threats of a changing world, as in the Marie-Emil action.

By presenting Alexandra with a series of temptations, Cather prepares the reader for a redefinition of love in the Alexandra-Carl action. In her dreams Alexandra feels the attraction of a romantic release from responsibility for self, "of being lifted up bodily and carried lightly by some one very strong" (p. 206). Significantly, Alexandra's dream of romantic love synthesizes maintenance and progression, for she dreams of her lover in pioneer images of the land's transcendence: "It was a man, certainly, who carried her, but he was like no man she knew; he was much larger and stronger and swifter, and he carried her as easily as if she were a sheaf of wheat. She never saw him, but, with eyes closed, she could feel that he was yellow like the sunlight, and there was the smell of ripe cornfields about him" (p. 206).

In her redefinition of love, Alexandra rejects romantic passion on several levels. First, she instinctively reacts to her dreams by punishing her body, bathing in cold water as if in penance. Second, she gradually formulates a question about romantic love. After visiting Frank in prison, Alexandra reflects, "It seemed unreasonable that life should have landed him in such a place as this." Then, looking for an explanation for this injustice, she asks, "And why, with [Marie's] happy, affectionate nature, should she have brought destruction and sorrow to all who had loved her. . . . Was there, then, something wrong in being warm-hearted and impulsive like that?" (p. 296). Third, and most important, Alexandra reaches a positive rejection of romantic love in her relationship with Carl: "I think we shall be very happy. I haven't any fears. I think when friends marry, they are safe. We don't suffer like—those young ones" (p. 308).

In the concluding passage of *O Pioneers!*, Alexandra synthesizes the transendent and immanent elements in herself. She continues her pioneer definition of herself in terms of the land, a definition that contrasts sharply to the romantic definition of self in terms of another person. As Carl says to Alexandra, "You belong to the land . . . as you have always said. Now more than ever" (p. 307). Her synthesis is possible, perhaps, because Cather does not develop integration with society as an issue in the novel. Both psychologically (she is a fierce individualist) and physically (on the farm, she is isolated from society), Alexandra remains independent from society.

With this final testimony to the universals that comprise the only valid frame of reference, Cather completes her characterization of Alexandra as a complex, fully human person. Cather is explicit that Alexandra's development is possible because she has not defined herself within traditional sexist roles. When Alexandra and Emil see a wild duck, alone, swimming on a river, Cather reflects, "Most of Alexandra's happy memories were as impersonal as this one; yet to her they were very personal. Her mind was a white book with clear writing about weather and beasts and growing things. Not many people would have cared to read it; only a happy few. She had never been in love, she had never indulged in sentimental reveries. Even as a girl she had looked upon men as work-fellows" (p. 205).

After *O Pioneers!*, Cather left the pioneer woman to portray Thea Kronborg who, in *The Song of the Lark*, attempts to define value through dedication to transcendence. But Cather returns to the pioneer woman in *My Ántonia*. With Ántonia Shimerda, Cather presents the pioneer woman who represents the value of maintenance. Unlike Alexandra, Ántonia does not realize universals through her relationship with the land, and, unlike Thea, Ántonia does not realize universals through her art. Instead, by the traditional woman's role of bearing and raising children, Ántonia provides the immanence necessary for other characters to achieve transcendence. As a result, *My Ántonia* is not about Ántonia so much as it is about what an archetypal pioneer woman may offer to others, here represented by the narrator, Jim Burden.

In *My Ántonia*, Cather separates the immanent and the transcendent elements described in *O Pioneers!* By this separation, Cather distances herself and the reader from Ántonia. We are removed from Ántonia because of the narrative lens of the novel supplied by Jim Burden. But we are distanced from Ántonia also because there is virtually no dramatic characterization of her. It is not what Ántonia does that is developed—in fact, she does very little; instead, it is what she is, especially to Jim, that is essential. Jim Burden's use of the possessive *my* in the title points the way to the thematic focus of the book.

In plot development, Cather similarly uses possessives to portray alternatives for a pioneer woman who functions as a woman. The young Ántonia is Mr. Shimerda's daughter; then, upon the death of her father, she is Ambrosch's sister, treated like a possession when "Ambrosch hired his sister out like a man" (p. 147); when she is preparing to leave home to work in town, he barters for wages from her. In town, she is Harlings' Tony; she prepares to leave town by becoming Larry Donovan's girl. When she is deserted by Larry Donovan, she is referred to as "poor Tony," for she no longer has a primary relationship with a man. Finally, she is redeemed by becoming Cuzak's wife. Throughout this progression, Ántonia plays an essentially passive role. She does not consciously define her own destiny, as did Alexandra Bergson. Ántonia's passivity is illustrated when she marries, for only Cuzak's choice of Ántonia is described: "When he began to look about, he saw Ántonia, and she was exactly the kind of girl he had always been looking for" (p. 365). There is no comparable passage relating decision or choice by Ántonia.

Similarly, Cather separates the transcendent from the immanent elements in the primary relationship of the novel, between Ántonia and Jim Burden. Thematically, Ántonia complements the narrator, Jim. Together they illustrate the conventional relations between the sexes: Ántonia is in the passive position, admiring Jim's active involvement in life. Cather depicts Jim's discomfort acutely when Ántonia does not fit the role he assumes for a woman: "She was four years older than I, to be sure, and had seen more of the world; but I was a boy and she was a girl, and I resented her protecting manner. Before the autumn was over, she began to treat me more like an equal and to defer to me in other things than reading lessons" (p. 43). For the girl Ántonia to be an equal with him, she must defer to him.

Throughout the novel, Ántonia remains for Jim a touchstone of stability with pioneer values. We see in Jim an outward expansion as he moves from the isolated farm to town; from the town to the university at Lincoln; from Lincoln to Harvard, and from Harvard to cosmopolitan centers of the world. In contrast, Ántonia rejects such a movement. She belongs on the farm; her one move into town is almost disastrous for her. By her constancy, Ántonia provides the immanence that may support expansive souls' movement into universals. The adult Jim returns to Ántonia and articulates this value: "She lent herself to immemorial human attitudes which we recognize by instinct as universal and true" (p. 353). More specifically, Ántonia acts to stimulate creative impulses in others, for "she still had that something which fires the imagination, could still stop one's breath for a moment by a look or gesture that somehow revealed the meaning in common things" (p. 353). Her realities are her children, and, among them her sons are the real testimony to her accomplishment. The final chapter is titled "Cuzak's boys"; Ántonia and her daughters are significantly missing. And Jim's tribute to Ántonia is through her sons: "It is no wonder that her sons stood tall and straight. She was a rich mine of life, like the founders of early races" (p. 353).

As the archetypal woman, Ántonia offers constant, unquestioning love.

The refrain that Ántonia could never see any bad in someone she loved runs like a motif throughout the book. With her children, she is a natural mother: like the land, she insures that nature and life will continue. Through her, pioneer values are transmitted to future generations. Her daughter, Martha, is like Ántonia; she is teaching her younger daughter, Anna, to be like her (p. 343). To Jim, she is inspiration; as he declares to her, "I'd have liked to have you for a sweetheart, or a wife, or my mother or sister—anything that a woman can be to a man. The idea of you is a part of my mind; you influence my likes and dislikes, all my tastes, hundreds of times when I don't realize it. You really are a part of me" (p. 321). Knowledge of such women prepares the active mind for a world of ideas: "It came over me, as it had never done before, the relation between girls like those and the poetry of Virgil. If there were no girls like them in the world, there would be no poetry" (p. 270).

Cather recognizes that Ántonia represents a necessary, vital value. Yet through *My Ántonia*, Cather develops tension against the very constancy that is Ántonia's strength. The other hired girls, developing in direct opposition to Ántonia, are in some ways more interesting than Ántonia; in fact, Cather allows Ántonia to drop out of sight for a portion of the novel while she concentrates upon Lena Lingard. One suspects that Cather sympathizes with Jim who, by the end of *My Ántonia*, describes this tension when he talks with Cuzak. Cuzak is "a city man" who "liked theatres and lighted streets and music and a game of dominoes after the day's work was over" and who plies Jim with "a great many questions about [Jim's] trip through Bohemia, about Vienna and the Ringstrasse and the theatres" (p. 366). Finally, Jim wonders about the cost to Cuzak of marriage to Ántonia: "It did rather seem to me that Cuzak had been made the instrument of Ántonia's special mission. This was a fine life, certainly, but it wasn't the kind of life he had wanted to live. I wondered whether the life that was right for one was ever right for two!" (p. 367).

The questions raised by Jim define the tension against the stable, constant values represented by the pioneer woman, Ántonia: just as characters move outward, away from Ántonia, so does time move on, leaving first generation pioneers behind. Significantly, Ántonia Shimerda is Cather's last great pioneer woman. After *My Ántonia*, Cather leaves first generation pioneers to concentrate upon the transference of pioneer values to the modern age, despite the fact that the frontier stimulus for those values has been lost. The tragedy of her last great female characters—most notably Marian Forrester and Myra Henshawe—results from the disparity between their potential for greatness and their inability to translate that potential into action. In *O Pioneers!* and *My Ántonia*, Cather left for us two examples of such a translation—Alexandra, who synthesized the traditional pioneer male qualities of expansive movement with the traditional pioneer female ones of stability; and Ántonia, who, by the stability of her personal pioneer qualities, offered expansive movement to others. The achievement of Willa Cather's pioneer women, finally, is that through this expansive movement, the characters become greater than their types: they transcend their pioneer setting and their feminine roles, representing universal values characteristic of the most fully human activities.

NOTES

1. For a summary of criticism on Cather, see "Willa Cather," by Bernice Slote, in *Fifteen Modern American Authors: A Survey of Research and Criticism*, ed. Jackson R. Bryer (Durham, North Carolina: Duke Univ. Press, 1969), esp. pp. 32-61.
2. See Simone de Beauvoir's discussion of this duality in *The Second Sex*, trans. and ed. H. M. Parshley (1953; rpt. New York: Vintage, 1974), p. 480.
3. Ruth Yeazell, "Fictional Heroines and Feminist Critics," *Novel*, 8 (Fall, 1974), 29.
4. In *My Ántonia*, Jim Burden describes this process: "I was something that lay under the sun and felt it, like the pumpkins, and I did not want to be anything more. I was entirely happy. Perhaps we feel like that when we die and become a part of something entire, whether it is sun and air, or goodness and knowledge. At any rate, that is happiness; to be dissolved into something complete and great. When it comes to one, it comes as naturally as sleep" (Sentry edition; Boston: Houghton Mifflin, 1961), p. 18. Subsequent references to this edition will appear in the text.

The Idioms and Figures of *Cheyenne Autumn*

PAM DOHER

Pam Doher teaches in the English department at Kearney State College, Kearney, Nebraska.

Beneath the easy, flowing rhythms and simple vocabulary of Mari Sandoz's *Cheyenne Autumn* (New York: Avon, 1964) lies an intricate and complex pattern of language. To communicate some of the mystic beauty of Cheyenne life and culture, Sandoz employs such tropes as metaphor, metonymy, simile, synecdoche, and personification. These terms of classical rhetoric, however, fade into the background when one reads *Cheyenne Autumn*, for it is not the classical mastery of these devices which is amazing, but the naturalness with which Sandoz employs them. Sandoz herself, in the Preface to *Cheyenne Autumn*, calls these devices "the idiom and the figures of Cheyenne life," and says that the purpose behind them is "to convey something of these deep, complex, patterned interrelationships" between the Cheyenne people, their land, and the time (pp. vii-viii). In view of this express purpose, then, a most rewarding approach to *Cheyenne Autumn* develops if Sandoz's use of figurative language is regarded not as a list of technical classical devices which would have little meaning to the actual characters of the book, but as a natural outgrowth and reflection of the land and the people involved.

Even a general discussion of basic mechanical considerations in *Cheyenne Autumn* points out the natural relationship of the language to the Indian people. Though not written from a first person point of view, *Cheyenne Autumn* definitely presents the Indian point of view. When the omniscient narrator does descend into a character to voice his or her thoughts and feelings, most often that single character is a Cheyenne such as Little Wolf or Spotted Deer. Naturally, the world as seen through the eyes of a Cheyenne becomes a Cheyenne world, described in Cheyenne terms. The basic concretes, or images, for the comparisons drawn for Sandoz's metaphors and similes (the most common figurative devices in the book) come from the life of the Cheyenne: the animals he sees, his possessions, and his land. The vocabulary becomes the non-technical vocabulary of a non-technical people, simple and uncomplicated. Sandoz very carefully avoids anachronisms, using only the actual elements of Cheyenne life in the late 1800's. In an effort to match the language to the lifestyle, Sandoz makes the environment her richest source of imagery.

Not only the physical environment, but also the cultural environment shapes the basis of Sandoz's work. Many of the idioms are related to the customs and traditions of the Cheyenne. For example, the Cheyenne believe that death is a return to the earth and that when the men mourn for a dead loved one they use the earth as a sign of mourning. So at the death of Black Beaver, when the men literally "let their hair stream loose with earth and grass in it," the women, in Sandoz's figurative sense, also use the earth, their keening "rising like a sorrowful dust" (p. 73). Another Cheyenne custom here is for the people to draw their robes or blankets to their eyes to hide sorrow or anger which might be seen in their faces. Hence Sandoz speaks of "blankets of anger" or "sorrowful blankets." In some figures, customs and environment come together. Camp fires, for instance, represent the physical warmth and good things of the environment. The absence or inaccessability of a camp fire represents evil or discomfort. According to custom, if someone brings bad news to the camp, he stands back from the fire, thus indicating the nature of his information. If someone is in deep despair he turns his back to the fire. So when events unfavorable to the Cheyenne occur, Sandoz often describes them in relation to the camp fire. The Cheyenne were forced to move to the distasteful Indian Territory "before the children were warmed on both sides" and, after the Robinson outbreak, Hog's wounded daughter, a prisoner at the fort, lies "close to the fire, her face almost in it, as though she could never be warmed again" with so many of her people lost, dying, or dead.

Another Cheyenne cultural concept which gives rise to figurative language is that of the oneness and flow of life and time. In setting the pace of *Cheyenne Autumn*, Sandoz often overlaps or combines the literary concepts of scene and summary, thus reflecting the Cheyenne perception of time as an "eternal stream . . . in which man, the tree, the rock, the cloud, and all the other things were simultaneously in all the places they had ever been; and all things that had ever been in a place were always in the present there, in the being and occurring" (p. vii). So in the middle of a scene, Sandoz may summarize all the important events that have happened at a certain place, such as the Sappa River, or to a certain person, such as Brave One. The places and events then, by association, become the basic elements of such figures as "the sorrow of the Sappa" or the "hungry pots" of Indian Territory. To further demonstrate this concept of flow (or, as she terms it, "continuality"), Sandoz repeatedly uses many of the same images throughout the book. Rarely does she use an image once and then drop it. Some of the more common images, such as the buffalo, the bear, and the moccasin, may contain slightly different implications from one use to another, but the basic meaning remains constant. The buffalo may be big and powerful and dark, but the crucial characteristic is that the buffalo serves as the main source of food, shelter, and life for the Cheyenne. Thus things which are harmful to the buffalo, such as white settlers and railroads, are also harmful to the Indian. Sandoz may develop many characteristics of a concrete image to further the complexity of interrelationships in Cheyenne life. She also weaves strands of separate images together to further strengthen the pattern of relations. Through the first two-thirds of *Cheyenne Autumn*, for instance, Sandoz sets up the image of the grizzly bear as mighty and powerful. Little Wolf in his anger fights "not like a man at all but like a grizzly bear, fierce, fearless, ready to lunge, to slash and claw" (p. 107). At the same time she sets up the field mouse as weak, powerless and fearful. In their secret escape from Indian Territory, the Cheyenne people run as "silent as field mice" and later "scatter like mice under leaves" for safety in the rough country. The constant and separate repetition of these two images, mouse and bear, creates a linear unity in the book, but a more complex pattern occurs when the two are brought together towards the end. "And now there were signals of new soldiers coming close, many more soldiers out, to reach for the Cheyennes like a great grizzly clawing at the rocks for hidden mice" (p. 257). Such combinations form a pattern of language as the people themselves form a pattern of life, unifying the work, and maintaining the point of view. To gain a greater appreciation of the figurative language, however, one must look at "the idiom and the figures" not only as extensions of basic literary concepts but also as elements of Cheyenne life.

Sandoz selects one group of images from the possessions of the Cheyenne. Since the stature of a Cheyenne was often judged by the quality and quantity of his belongings, this set of images figures prominently in *Cheyenne Autumn*. Fittingly, weapons of war describe warlike encounters. During the heat violence of the argument preceding the separation of Dull Knife and Little Wolf, Sandoz compares Little Wolf's voice with the sharpness of a Cheyenne battle ax and says that the tempers of the men were "taut as dry bowstrings," tautness and dryness being required of a bowstring in battle. Attacks by both whites and Cheyennes strike at their victims "like lance heads." Less warlike possessions, such as robes and blankets, physically represent warmth and comfort, figuratively represent concealment or safety. Sandoz compares the fog after the separation of the tribe to a blanket for hiding shame; in the flight, the Cheyenne people hide in blankets of fog and shadow, hide from blankets of bullets; distasteful bad news sits on Tangle Hair "like the moldy robe of bereavement, of banishment"; and the bloodletting of a sundance Sandoz likens to "a great red blanket spread upon the ground to plead for a vision to save the people" (p. 139). Even the bundles in which the Cheyenne carry their possessions become figurative elements, when the sick and tired people look like sacks of bones or drop "like worthless bundles" to the ground.

One of the most frequent images of *Cheyenne Autumn* belongs in this category of possessions, its importance being that it expresses at one time or another nearly all phases of Cheyenne life. The idiom of the moccasin occurs so frequently as representative of the people that it becomes a study in itself. As might be expected, the moccasin often describes the movement of the Cheyenne. Leaving a camp, "the moccasins began to move again"; in quiet movement Sandoz describes the moccasin as a whisper compared with the war hoops of horses' hoofs; to hurry the people is "to hasten the moccasins." Along with the movement of the people, the moccasin also indicates direction, physical and spiritual. When the Indians set out for a physical place, Sandoz says they "point their moccasins," and Little Wolf, sensing defeat, becomes "certain that the old ways had to be forgotten, the moccasins on a new path." The moccasin can express good as in land "where the earth grew under the moccasin"; but more often, in keeping with the desperate situation of the Cheyenne, the moccasin expresses sorrowful events, the condition of the moccasin indicating the condition of the people. The Cheyenne want to leave Indian Territory because "in this small hungry place we must stand on the moccasins of our brothers" (p. 27). Evils such as the soldiers' guns are "long shadows across the moccasin toe." In anger, Dull Knife tells Little Wolf, "Too long your tongue has been the thorn in my moccasin!" (p. 149), and to Little Finger Nail a bad thought troubles him as a thorn in his moccasin would trouble him. In sickness and danger the Cheyenne "go with their moccasin in the cactus." A hungry man must have fast moccasins and the Cheyenne must have horses to get their moccasins out of the cactus, to carry them and their possessions to safety.

Another important group of figures in *Cheyenne Autumn* deals with the land, the environment in which the Cheyenne find themselves. Since the Cheyenne lived in close communion with their land, this category supplies Sandoz with an inexhaustible source of figurative material, covering all phases of Cheyenne life and indicating their mystic belief in the oneness of all beings and things. From birth, when a Cheyenne "puts a foot upon the grass" until death when he returns to the grass or to the earth, the land plays a governing role in his life. Consequently, the characteristics found in the earth are often found in him. Little Wolf can be solid as a mountain and yet see his people fall apart "like sandstone struck by a great hammer." The Cheyenne can have "the strength of stone in their faces" yet feel "the weight of bereavement upon them like a stone in the breast" until their hearts could break "like a rock in frost." Something fated appears as "a decision already marked in the dust"; something fated like knowing that someday each of them must "go to the burial rocks." Until that time they will be as reflections of the earth: like Bridge, "the water of his eyes running down the gullied old face" (p. 56) in thankfulness; like Black Horse, his face "like a dark bluff washed by rain" (p. 123) in sorrow; like the wounded Sitting Man, "with blood gushing around [the bone] like a welling spring" (p. 77) in pain. For many the only relief possible comes in the little hole at Warbonnet, their "bodies piled like gray, bloody sacks of earth thrown this way and that upon each other" (p. 286), kin to the soil even in death.

A natural outgrowth of the earth imagery, trees stand as a major figure in the language of land and environment. Trees, too, Sandoz uses to express both good times and bad times for the Cheyenne. Early in their flight, early in the battles, the Cheyenne are "like many colored bushes and tree tips in their warbonnets and feathered lances along the crest of the hills" (p. 62); making escape talks to his captured people on the way to Robinson, Hog is "a powerful figure, looking tall as a great winter pine." Black Beaver, however, is killed by the white man and they leave him "naked like an uprooted brown tree fallen beside the trail" (p. 73); and at the Sappa the whites "threw everybody into the fire, like big trees and little trees" (p. 137). Much as the trees, the Cheyenne grow, become diseased, and die. Confined at Fort Robinson, Left Hand feels "the power of his hunting arm useless here as a dying branch" (p. 222), and the disheartened Cheyenne are as gray and lifeless as dead leaves. Again a deeper pattern of relationships emerges when Sandoz combines images, describing the earth in terms of the trees. "The White River valley lay like a bending, snow-covered leaf in the October sun, the midrib the frozen stream, the veins the little creeks and drifted canyons that reached far out to the higher prairie on each side" (p. 209). Once more the combination of images adds to the unity and complexity of Sandoz's language pattern. *Cheyenne Autumn* stretches out like a stream to follow and explore, each chapter of frozen time a leaf on the dying tree called Cheyenne.

As elements of the physical environment, wind and weather strongly influence Sandoz's Cheyenne idiom. From "friendly clouds" which hide the escaping Cheyenne to blizzards which freeze them, the Cheyenne see it all. Quite often the weather idiom takes the form of a storm, showing strong emotion. When a falling out takes place among the Cheyenne, Sandoz terms it a cold wind blowing up between them. At such emotional times, voices can become as angry as a blizzard and eyes as cold as the blizzard wind. For Little Wolf, the weather idiom comes naturally to the tongue in voicing his anger at trouble makers. He tells them, "We need less thunder in the mouth and more lightning in the hand if we are to escape to the north and save the helpless ones with us" (p. 49). Of course storms also fit into figures about battle. In one battle the noise is like a rolling hailstorm, and in another "The bullets drove the sand upon the Indians like frozen sleet whipped by a blizzard; the thunder of the Gatling guns hammered the shaking earth" (p. 117). Further figurative use of the wind demonstrates the deep sense of loss the Cheyenne feel. The voices of those who would speak in favor of the Cheyenne are "like the wind on the buffalo grass," as are the white promises. Little Wolf knows he must lead his people to safety or they will "lie scattered and lost forever on the wind." All manner of winds find their way into *Cheyenne Autumn*. In the face of contagious disease the lodges of the Cheyenne fall as though blown down by a great wind, and in despair the Cheyenne men are ready to fight even each other over any trifle, "at the flutter of a wind." A powerful wind of laughter very early blows away Yellow Wolf's words of peace, but when Hog later rips up a newspaper clipping predicting their removal to Indian Territory and throws the pieces "like unclean feathers to the wind," he realizes the bad words cannot be blown away so easily. Still, during times of strife when others speak out against him, Hog maintains his composure and Sandoz says it is "as though the wind carried only its own noise." But that in itself forms a grave burden for both the Cheyenne and his land, since the noise of the encroaching white man keeps adding its new and deathly weight to everything he touches.

Just as important to Cheyenne idiom as the wind and trees are the animals of Sandoz's figures. The actions of the Cheyenne often resemble the actions of some other creature of the land, and Sandoz most often notes these characteristics in metaphors and similes. When the Indians are happy and free their motions and emotions soar like great flying things, eagles and hawks; but in times of fear and danger some hide like quail in the grass, some act as decoys like a mother quail protecting her young, others flush and run as frightened young quail are wont to do. Times of plenty appear in figures such as "fat as prairie dogs" or "fat as fall buffalo"; but in times of hunger and poverty the Indians' bodies are "as melted of fat as hibernating bears." The whole horrible story of the Indian flight can be told using only the figures involving animals. As they begin the journey the Cheyennes move like the sly coyote in the shadows. They are deadly as a hungry wolf and as determined as the wolf on the scent of a newborn calf. When forced to fight, they dig like badgers and hide in the rifle pits like prairie dogs. If cornered they fight fiercely, like a grizzly bear or some other great wounded animal. Caught in the open they scatter like mice or prairie chickens; surrounded, their fright is that of the frantic elk or antelope. Finally, those who escape sleep like worn-out buffalo; those caught are crushed like rabbits and bugs or butchered like fleeing buffalo. The figure of the dying buffalo holds an especially meaningful position because the end of the great herds of buffalo signals, figuratively and literally, the end of the Plains Indians' greatness. The fate of animal and man are tightly joined in the actions, customs, and religion of the Indian. Deliberately the whites destroy the buffalo and so the Indian; deliberately Sandoz points this out by using the buffalo, dead, dying, and absent, as her most frequent animal image.

Another thread of idioms tied to the fate of the Cheyenne involves images of decay and entrapment. The "moldy robe of bereavement, of banishment" is perhaps the most fitting image of the sadness, hard times, and death forced upon a people being driven from their own land. The paths the Cheyenne walk no longer afford life and freedom. Instead, the wind is full of decay and everywhere "the bleaching bones lay white as morning frost." Only the bones of man and animal remain to tell of good times now gone. Many of these figurative passages demonstrate the destruction of Indian and nature while linking that destruction with the progress of the whites. "Bleaching bones lay all around, the ribs standing naked as the wagon bows of the settlers who drove their shining plows where the great dark herds had grazed even two years ago" (p.23). In reflection of nature's disruption and decay, Sandoz likens the Indian people to dead leaves and dying branches, and in winter frostbite on the children is "darkened and puffed as spoiled patches on a pumpkin." The Cheyenne and the earth itself fall apart under the blows of progress, both crumbling like stones hit by a great hammer. Seeing the collapse of his world, one Cheyenne says while in the Indian Territory, "Today we are only a crumbling sand bar in the spring Platte, with the flood waters rising all around" (p. 26). Surrounded by a swift-moving river of whites, the Cheyenne have no open routes left to them. Their world has decayed beyond control and recovery.

As this truth dawns on the Cheyenne, Sandoz includes more images of isolation and entrapment. At Robinson, Dull Knife's band feels "really cut off, like a small bunch of buffaloes in a tribal surround" (p. 180). Red Cloud offers no real assistance to them for his own tribe is "shut in by a forest of guns." Some disheartened Indians turn inward, their solitude as complete as being "shut away in a cave." As surrounds, encirclements, and closing attacks become more frequent, the smoke of the soldier guns seems like creeping walls moving against the Cheyenne; the battle line of the whites is "like a solid wall pushing in until the people became very excited, afraid because this time they could not run." Still the whites keep pushing, keep tightening their grip, killing the buffalo, killing the Indian, until very little is left of the good land the Cheyenne once knew. The whites want it all, no matter what changes they must make. They will not put down their arms and accept the Indian, mix and become one with him "like the bullets of enemies heated in the same lead kettle." Instead they destroy the Indian culture and way of life, tearing away even at his pride until his movements must be "like the fox sneaking up a gully, not like the

Cheyennes of the old days, bold as the gray wolf who stalks the ridge with his tail straight up in the air" (p. 37). So the whites press their unwelcome presence upon the land and upon the Cheyenne.

A final way Sandoz's idioms and figures characterize the Cheyenne is through contrast with the whites. Sandoz represents the Cheyenne as the people of nature and of the land, living by their instincts as the wolf and the buffalo do. The whites of *Cheyenne Autumn*, however, seem to have lost contact with many of their instincts concerning the land. Like their sheep, the whites are silly, tame animals. Similarly, the white man's cattle have lost the natural fear of man and may be easily herded, unlike the wild buffalo of the Indian. Physical descriptions of the Cheyenne are in terms of the earth, with the people like mountains, bluffs, trees, and animals. They are free to be themselves, none giving orders or commands. The description of the advanced whites, on the other hand, often reflects their technology and tools. They are pale as old paper and their soldiers not only take orders, but are "like their bullet molds that serve one purpose and then are folded away until another time" (p. 98). The whites lack not only the freedom of the Indian warriors but also the Cheyennes' mystic relation to the earth, a relationship already witnessed in an abundance of Cheyenne idiom and figures. To the whites the land is more of a tool or a possession than a living thing, a fact readily apparent in the absence of Sandoz's flowing figurative language in the few chapters and scenes written from a white viewpoint.

The frequent associations of the Cheyenne with buffalo, eagle, wolf, and so on, portray him as noble, powerful, and admirable. At times, in cases of desperation, the Cheyenne may be linked with mice, quail and other lower life forms, but he still may be regarded higher than the white man whose most frequent animal associations are with the lowest forms of crawling life. The spider serves as the most obvious "animal" association to the white man since the same Cheyenne word, *veho*, denotes both *spider* and *white man*. The treachery of the whites is like the "trick of the spider. . . . The *veho* has long spun his web for the feet of those who have wings but are too foolish to fly . . . " (p. 18). The Cheyenne wait too long to fly, to try to regain all that was once theirs, and the telegraph, "the talking wire, like spider ropes," helps ensnare them. Still in the insect vein, Sandoz repeatedly compares the whites and their wagon trains to "dark strings of ants hurrying before the winter." Then again, still as low crawling life, the whites' wagons appear as a long gray worm, their railroad as a great watchful snake, their soldier columns as a dark, angry, twisting snake in the dust. " 'The man who looks one place and plants the moccasin in another may tread on a rattlesnake,' Bridge, the old medicine healer, said" (p. 51). Indeed, the Cheyenne who trusts the white men against his own better judgement eventually realizes the truth of Bridge's words and feels the pain of the white man's vicious bite. Towards the end, however, neither the whites nor the Indians retain any great metaphorical status, for as the Cheyenne numbers dwindle, so do the images and figures, until the once-sparkling flow of life and words is reduced to a stagnant puddle.

Seen in Sandoz's own simple terms as "the idiom and the figures of Cheyenne life," the figurative language of *Cheyenne Autumn* aptly depicts the unity, the "continuality," and the desperation of the Cheyenne and their land. The rhythmic beauty of Sandoz's figures of speech captures much of the oneness and the mystic quality of the people. The detail and the complex simplicity of Sandoz's language remain an intriguing and understanding picture of the Cheyenne people. Any final description of Mari Sandoz's accomplishment in *Cheyenne Autumn* must read like her own description of the Cheyenne:

> Both [Great Eyes and Left Hand] were grandfathers now and between them they tied these people together like beads of two colors, one from each side, woven into an intricate, beautiful Cheyenne pattern (p. 141).

Cheyenne Autumn, too, is such a pattern.

Neihardt, Momaday, and the Art of Indian Autobiography

WILLIAM BLOODWORTH

William Bloodworth is associate professor of English at East Carolina University. His book on Upton Sinclair has just been published by Twayne, and he is now at work on a study of popular western novels from Wister to Haycox.

American Indian autobiographies present a peculiar problem when they are considered as a distinct literary form. The peculiarity of the problem lies in the fact that autobiography as we know it—telling the story of one's life—involves assumptions of intellectual individualism that have few counterparts in native American culture. The development of autobiography as a literary genre is also directly related to the development of writing (with autobiographies, like Franklin's, sometimes beginning as personal correspondence) and print. In fact, the safe distance that print media puts between speaker and audience promotes the introspective and ego-conscious qualities of many autobiographies. Most importantly, autobiography reflects a cultural situation—that of modern European and American civilization—which allows individuals to explore and even celebrate the ways in which their lives depart from traditional patterns.

In traditional native American culture, however, autobiography as a form of expression is limited mainly to coup stories, stories that explain an individual's name, and narrative elements in oratory and prophecy. Whatever individualism these expressions imply is a matter of personal, and mainly male, achievement in traditional tribal activities (war, hunting, religion). Furthermore, they are generally intended to serve specific, pragmatic functions, such as establishing a warrior's bravery, and they never attempt to present the speaker's whole life. In a pamphlet on Plains Indian autobiography, Lynn Woods O'Brien points out that entire life stories were not told among the tribes of the Plains because "the lives of tribal members did not vary enough from one another to warrant a complete recital. Tribes were homogeneous cultural units in which the basic patterns of daily life were the same for all."[1] Autobiography, with its emphasis on understanding or celebrating the individual, could not become a major form of expression in a cultural setting devoted to tribal values and traditional behavior patterns.

Yet Indian autobiographies do exist, and they constitute a small but significant part of western American literature which has received little critical attention. Many of the published autobiographies of native Americans are the result of anthropological fieldworkers, oral historians and other white scholars, or western travelers and military figures interested in Indian culture. Autobiographies of this kind should perhaps be called "life histories," with the *auto* part of the narratives played down and the factual information within them emphasized. Often they take the form of repetitive coup stories—these being a familiar kind of Indian expression—dealing with pre-reservation life. Such life histories deserve to be evaluated primarily on the grounds of their historical and anthropological content, not their literary qualities.

Some Indian autobiographies, considerably fewer in number than the life histories, are genuine literary efforts. That is, they stress the form of expression as well as content, their ends are both artistic and informative, and they appeal to a wide audience including non-Indian and non-specialist readers. In this paper I wish to discuss three works that are Indian in content, autobiographical in form, and literary in purpose. One is *Black Elk Speaks*, the classic "Life Story of a Holy Man of the Oglala Sioux" which John G. Niehardt published in 1932. This book represents the telling of an Indian's personal story through the efforts of a sympathetic and talented white writer; it is also typical in its focus on pre-reservation Indian life. In these respects, *Black Elk Speaks* serves as a distinct contrast to the other two works discussed here. *The Way to Rainy Mountain* (1969) and *The Names* (1976) both by N. Scott Momaday, represent the efforts of an enormously talented contemporary Indian writer who needs no assistance from white friends and who focuses on both the pre-reservation life of his Kiowa ancestors and his own life as an "assimilated" twentieth-century Indian.

The unifying link between Neihardt's presentation of Black Elk's life and Momaday's autobiographical writings is an attempt to remain true to the facts and the spirit of Indian culture while, at the same time, appealing to a general audience composed mainly of white readers. The difficulty here lies in the apparent contradiction between the intellectual individualism inherent in written autobiography and the tribalism of Indian culture. In other words, the art of Indian autobiography must attempt to reconcile the discrepancy between its cultural content and its literary form. Neihardt and Momaday offer two different practices of this art, one by emphasizing vision and the other by emphasizing the oral traditions of myth, legend, and story.

It is hardly necessary to dwell upon the literary and popular reputations of *Black Elk Speaks*. As Blair Whitney points out in his recent book on Neihardt, *Black Elk Speaks* "received praise from every reviewer" when it was published in 1932, became a college classic in the sixties when it was reissued by the University of Nebraska Press, and "can now be found in almost any bookstore."[2] However, it may still be necessary to explain the respective roles of Black Elk and John Neihardt in the making of the book. *Black Elk Speaks* is no simple translation,nor is it a typical ghost-written autobiography. Rather, as Sally McKluskey was careful to point out when the book became widely popular in 1972, Neihardt's function was "both creative and editorial."[3] In 1930 and 1931 he had interviewed Black Elk, a *wichasha wakan* or holy man of the Oglala Sioux who had taken part in the 1890 Ghost Dances. Black Elk apparently sensed that Neihardt was the appropriate white man to hear his story, and he gave it to the white poet through a translator over a period of several months. Neihardt fashioned the book from over 400 pages of typed transcripts. His main intention, he said, was "to re-create in English the mood and manner of the old man's narrative. This was often a grueling and difficult task."[4] In a 1971 interview Neihardt said that "the translation—or rather the *transformation*—of what was given me was expressed so that it could be understood by the white world."[5] The end result is clearly Black Elk's autobiography, but it is just as clearly John Neihardt's book.

The effectiveness of *Black Elk Speaks* depends largely upon a careful orchestration of Sioux mysticism and the facts of physical and historical existence as they were felt by Plains Indians from the 1860s to the 1930s. In the preface to his original edition Neihardt explained that when he first met Black Elk in 1930 he was impressed by "the scope of the man's experience." Not only had Black Elk "lived the common life of his people in the good old times as well as in the tragic and heroic years of their final defeat and degradation," but "he had lived them in and for a world of higher values" and "seemed . . . to represent the consciousness of the Plains Indian more fully than any other I had ever known."[6] Consequently, the "Life Story" of Black Elk is structured around "the story of a mighty vision" (p. 1). Specifically, the vision is the one received by Black Elk at age nine, a spectacular revelation of his duty to unify his people, to restore the sacred hoop of the Sioux nation and make the sacred tree of life bloom again. In the book this vision determines Black Elk's purpose in life and, after parts of it are acted out in tribal ceremonies, transforms him into a *wichasha wakan*. But the book itself—or at least the telling of the story to Neihardt—represents the first time for Black Elk to reveal his entire vision. The autobiography, in its presentation of the vision, is thus a form of ceremony itself.

The manner in which Niehardt presents Black Elk's visionary experiences is his main effort at reconciling Indian culture with autobiography. Robert Sayre has explained at some length how the personal mysticism of Black Elk is not so much a matter of individual experience as it is a social phenomenon, both in its origins and in its uses. What appears to be a matter between the self and the gods is actually tribal and communal. In fact, Black Elk's great vision serves no purpose except anxiety until it is made public in ceremony.[7]

In addition to Sayre's point about the social context of the vision, we should note that Neihardt allows Black Elk to tell the intensely personal story of his inner life, but only in such a way as to refuse any credit or honor. Egotism is alien to the Sioux vision quest as Neihardt presents it. In Black Elk's first sentence the holy man makes it clear that he would not tell his story "if it were only the story of my life . . . for what is one man that he should make much of his winters, even when they bend him like a heavy snow?" What he must tell is the story of a vision "given to a man too weak to use it" (p. 1). The vision itself is what counts, not the man, because it represents "the Power of the World" whereas the individual is only "like a hole through which the power would come to the two-leggeds" (p. 209). When Black Elk mentions his power to heal, he says, "If I thought that I was doing it myself, the hole would close up and no power could come through" (p. 209).

Black Elk's story is quite the opposite of a success story, a typical mode of popular white autobiography. Not only does the book chart the tragic end of his people's way of life in such events as the killing of Crazy Horse and Sitting Bull, the slaughter at Wounded Knee, and the imprisoning of Indians in the ugly square cabins of reservation life, but it also bewails Black Elk's personal failure to live up to his vision. *Black Elk Speaks* can be read as a Sioux counterpart of *The Education of Henry Adams*, but with more faith in humanity remaining at the end of the story. Frustration dominates Black Elk's memory of his vision. Although the ceremonies he performs create a momentary sense of unity for his tribe, he is unable to restore the sacred hoop. He seems particularly regretful for having been deluded into following the ghost dance religion: "this was where I made my great mistake. I had had a very great vision. . . . But I followed the lesser visions that had come to me while dancing on Wounded Knee Creek" (pp. 253-54). And at the end of his account, following his descriptions of the events at Wounded Knee, he refers to himself as "now a pitiful old man who has done nothing, for the nation's hoop is broken and scattered. There is no center any longer, and the sacred tree is dead" (p. 276).

In addition to its treatment of visionary experience, *Black Elk Speaks* also remains faithful to Sioux culture by refusing to gloss over the unpleasant facts of Indian violence. In one instance, while telling of Custer's defeat, Black Elk mentions what happened when one of his cousins was badly wounded: "He was my cousin, and his father and my father were so angry over this, that they went out and butchered a Wasichu [a white] and cut him open. The Wasichu was fat, and his meat looked good to eat, but we did not eat any" (p. 131). This kind of candor—Neihardt's editorial refusal to bow entirely to sentimental white notions of Indian behavior—brings the reader back from "the world of higher values," humanizes Black Elk, and contributes a sense of honesty and objectivity to the book. But it does not supersede Neihardt's attention to vision.

In the autobiographical writings of N. Scott Momaday we have Indian autobiography that differs radically from that of *Black Elk Speaks* and from most other collected life histories of native Americans. The source of this difference is Momaday's own life, that of an unusually successful and well-assimilated Indian. Momaday was born on ancestral grounds in Oklahoma in 1934 (where his name was recorded on the Kiowa Indian Census Roll as Number 2035) and spent much of his early childhood there. However, his Kiowa father and his part-Cherokee mother, having made successful careers for themselves in art and education, taught Momaday English as his "native" language and later sent him off to Eastern schools. He was particularly influenced by his mother's love of English literature: "I have seen Grendel's shadow on the walls of Canyon de Chelly, and once, having led the sun around Hoskinini Mesa, I saw Copperfield at Oljeto Trading post."[8] Capitalizing on such advantages, Momaday has become a literary scholar, a professor at the University of California at Berkeley, a Pulitzer Prize winning novelist (with *House Made of Dawn* in 1968), and a widely-recognized poet. Although this kind of academic and literary achievement may disqualify Momaday as a genuine representative of traditional tribal Indian culture, it also indicates the unusual literary talent that Momaday brings to the practice of autobiography. Separated as he is by time, circumstance, and good fortune from "pure" Indian life, Momaday pays scant attention to mysticism or visionary experience. Instead, in both *The Way to Rainy Mountain* and *The Names* his writing involves a highly personal and often poetic articulation of remembered myths, legends, and family stories.

The Way to Rainy Mountain is not explicitly autobiographical. Yet it represents Momaday's attempt to fuse his personal and ancestral pasts into an imaginative whole. To do this Momaday makes use of three kinds of material: the first is Kiowa verbal tradition as expressed in myths and legends, the second is factual history, and the third is Momaday's own poetic response to remembered expressions and facts of Kiowa culture.

The Way to Rainy Mountain contains twenty-four numbered sections, and each section contains three items—one from myth or legend, one from history, and one from personal reflection. The sections themselves are divided into three groups: "The Setting Out," "The Going On," and "The Closing In." This progression follows Kiowa history from the tribe's seventeenth-century origins in the Northern Rockies to their nineteenth-century conquest of the Southern Plains to their eventual life on the Oklahoma reservation near Rainy Mountain in the Wichita Range. Momaday's method is clear in section I. The first item of the section relates the Kiowa coming-out myth, in which "the Kiowas came one by one into the world through a hollow log."[9] The second item shifts to history and offers a straightforward explanation of how the original names of the tribe meant "coming out." The final item tells of Momaday's own perceptions when he retraced the migration of his people and "came out" of the Rocky Mountain forests onto the expansive landscape of the High Plains:

> I could see the still, sunlit plain below, reaching away out of sight. At first there is no discrimination in the eye, nothing but the land itself, whole and impenetrable. But then smallest things begin to stand out of the depths—herds and rivers and groves—and each of these has perfect being in terms of distance and of silence and of age. Yes, I thought, now I see the earth as it really is; never will I see things as I saw them yesterday or the day before (p. 17).

Just as the emergence of the Kiowas from the mountains forever changed their culture, Momaday's imagination produces a permanent change in his attitudes.

In the freedom of its poetic associations, *The Way to Rainy Mountain* can be a difficult book to appreciate on first reading. "My major feelings are those of being cheated. I want to know a great deal more about the Kiowas," one of my students once wrote, with some justification, in an informal paper on Momaday's book. *The Way to Rainy Mountain* is an extremely personal statement, and at times even a sentimental one. It is a literary attempt by Momaday to discover and explore his Kiowa roots. In *The Names*, his later and more explicitly autobiographical book, he refers to what his mother did in her childhood and adolescence when she began to think of herself as an Indian despite the fact that her actual Indian blood was only that of a Cherokee great-grandmother: "That dim native heritage became a fascination and a cause for her. . . . She imagined who she was. This act of the imagination was, I believe, among the most important events of my mother's early life, as later the same essential act was to be among the most important of my own life" (p. 25). *The Way to Rainy Mountain* is the "essential act," or a large part thereof, which Momaday equates with his mother's effort at assuming an Indian identity, and the emphasis on personal imagination in the book is unmistakable. In section XXIV he offers a rationale for what he has been doing throughout his pages:

> Once in his life a man ought to concentrate his mind upon the remembered earth, I believe. He ought to give himself up to a particular landscape in his experience, to look at it from as many angles as he can, to wonder about it, to dwell upon it. He ought to imagine that he touches it with his hands at every season and listens to the sounds that are made upon it. He ought to imagine the creatures there and all the faintest motions of the wind. He ought to recollect the glare of noon and all the colors of the dawn and dusk (p. 83).

Momaday uses the verb *imagine* or its equivalents throughout this passage because, as he explains in his prologue, "The imaginative experience and the historical express equally the traditions of man's reality" (p. 4).

For Momaday in *The Way to Rainy Mountain* there are two kinds of imaginative experience. One is that embodied in the rich verbal tradition of his Kiowa ancestors, the tradition by which they "dared to imagine and determine who they were" (p. 4). The other is Momaday's own imagination which works *through* the verbal tradition of his people to recover and reestablish who he is.

In *The Names*, Momaday's most recent book, he also relies on the Kiowa verbal tradition for material and form, but in a less noticeable way. Primarily he models—or at least claims to model—his book on the way oral stories were told:

> In general my narrative is an autobiographical account. Specifically it is an act of the imagination. When I turn my mind to my early life, it is the imaginative part of it that comes first and irresistibly into reach, and of that part I take hold. This is one way to tell a story. In this instance it is my own way, and it is the way of my people. When Pohd-lohk told a story he began by being quiet. Then he said *Ah-keah-de*, "They were camping," and he said it every time. I have tried to write in the same spirit. Imagine: They were camping (prefatory note, n.p.).

Yet the book, complete with sepia-tone photographs of relatives and Momaday himself, looks like a typical autobiography and, in many places, reads like one. It involves a certain amount of celebration of self which reflects a compromise between the form of written autobiography and the nature of Indian culture. In spite of these things, however, the emphasis in the book is less on the individual whose autobiography it is than on the traditions and people that gave him existence and meaning.

This emphasis is implied in the title of the book and in the more or less central episode of Momaday's own naming. He was given the Kiowa name of Tsoai-talee ("Rock-Tree Boy") by his step great-grandfather, Pohd-lohk. *Tsoai* means "Rock Tree" and refers specifically to the Devil's Tower in Wyoming, a geological formation of sacred significance in Kiowa mythology:

> He took up the child in his hands and held it high, and he cradled it in his arms, singing to it and rocking it to and fro. With the others he passed the time of day, exchanged customary talk, scattered small exclamations on the air: Yes, yes. Quite so. So it is with us. But with the child he was deliberate, intent. And after a time all the other voices fell away, and his own grew up in their wake. It became monotonous and incessant, like a long running of the wind. The whole of the afternoon was caught up in it and carried along. Pohd-lohk spoke, as if telling a story, of the coming-out people, of their long journey. He spoke of how it was that everything began, of Tsoai, and of the stars falling or holding fast in strange patterns on the sky. And in this, at last, Pohd-lohk affirmed the whole life of the child in a name, saying: Now you are, Tsoai-talee (pp. 56-57).

Pohd-lohk, Momaday says earlier, "believed that a man's life proceeds from his name, in the way that a river proceeds from its source" (prefatory note). In *The Names* Momaday returns to his source through attention to his name, to the names of those he knew in childhood, white as well as red, and to the lives of those who bore the names. Significantly, the final passage of the book, in Momaday's always vivid and powerful prose, is an imagined return "with the eyes of my own mind" to the coming-out place of the Kiowas: "And then there were meadows full of wildflowers, and a mist roiled upon them, the slow, rolling spill of the mountain clouds. And in one of these, in a pool of low light, I touched the fallen tree, the hollow log there in the thin crust of the ice" (p. 167).

The Names abounds with scenes of childhood and adolescent imagination which chart the inner process of an Indian boy growing up in a largely white world. For instance, Momaday tells of his formative pre-adolescent years in Hobbs, New Mexico, during World War II, a period when he constantly imagined himself as a fighter pilot in the Pacific Theatre or as a football star on the local gridiron; he also devotes many pages to his adolescent years at the Jemez Pueblo where his mother and father ran the Jemez Day School for the Bureau of Indian Affairs. But consistently he draws attention to his Kiowa roots, the "old, sacred world" from which he had come. His pages are filled with references not only to the people whom he knew or had imagined, but also to the storytelling tradition passed on to him by his step great-grandfather and his father. While his mother read or made up stories for him, his father told "the old

Kiowa tales." "These were many times more exciting than anything I found at school; they, more than the grammars and arithmetics, nourished the life of my mind" (p. 88). Actually, the tales nourished his imagination, it seems, and Momaday's early acquaintance with the Kiowa way of imagining who they were—through storytelling and naming—was the source of his own literary ambitions.

John G. Neihardt (or, if we wish, some authorial hybrid of Neihardt and Black Elk) and Scott Momaday represent two important directions in literary Indian autobiography. Other directions have been taken, including the proud assertiveness of Luther Standing Bear. Lesser known recent expressions would include the explanatory and polemical statement of John Lame Deer and Richard Erdoes in *Lame Deer: Seeker of Visions* and the story of "learning about the world beyond hands' reach" offered by Emerson Blackhorse Mitchell and T. D. Allen in *Miracle Hill: The Story of a Navaho Boy.*[10] These and other personal stories deserve our attention for both historical and literary reasons. While autobiography may seem to be a form of expression that is somehow alien to native American themes and culture, the genre has been practiced with art and eloquence. This eloquence should continue, especially if native American writers continue to seek ways of reaffirming their traditional cultural values.

Notes

1. Lynn Woods O'Brien, *Plains Indian Autobiographies* (Boise: Boise State College, 1973), p. 5
2. Blair Whitney, *John G. Neihardt* (Boston: Twayne Publishers, 1976), pp. 90-91.
3. Sally McKluskey, "*Black Elk Speaks* and So Does John Neihardt," *Western American Literature*, 6 (Winter 1972), 237.
4. John G. Neihardt, *Black Elk Speaks* (New York: Pocket Books, 1971), p. xii. The statement is from the preface Neihardt wrote for this paperback edition.
5. As quoted in McKluskey, p. 238.
6. John G. Neihardt, *Black Elk Speaks* (New York: William Morrow, 1932), p. viii. The statement appears in the preface of the original edition. Other references to *Black Elk Speaks* are to this edition, and they are noted parenthetically.
7. Robert Sayre, "Vision and Experience in *Black Elk Speaks*," *College English*, 32 (February 1971), 509-35.
8. N. Scott Momaday, *The Names* (New York: Harper and Row, 1976), p. 60. Other references to this book are noted parenthetically.
9. N. Scott Momaday, *The Way to Rainy Mountain* (Albuquerque: Univ. of New Mexico Press, 1969), p. 16. This book is also available in a paperback edition published by Ballantine Books. Other references are noted parenthetically.
10. John Fire/Lame Deer and Richard Erdoes, *Lame Deer: Seeker of Visions* (New York: Simon and Schuster, 1972), and Emerson Blackhorse Mitchell and T. D. Allen, *Miracle Hill: The Story of a Navaho Boy* (Norman: Univ. of Oklahoma Press, 1967).